I0015815

Arduino

2 books in 1

The Master Guide to Learn Arduino Programming with Easy-To-Follow Methods, Tools And Strategies

By

Robert Campbell

© Copyright 2021 - All rights reserved.

This document is geared towards providing exact and reliable information regarding the topic and issue covered. The publication is sold with the idea that the publisher is not required to render accounting, officially permitted, or otherwise, qualified services. If advice is necessary, legal or professional, a practiced individual in the profession should be ordered from a Declaration of Principles, which was accepted and approved equally by a Committee of the American Bar Association and a Committee of Publishers and Associations.

In no way is it legal to reproduce, duplicate, or transmit any part of this document in either electronic means or printed format. Recording this publication is strictly prohibited, and any storage of this document is not allowed unless with written permission from the publisher. All rights reserved.

The information provided herein is stated to be truthful and consistent. In terms of inattention or otherwise, any liability, by any usage or abuse of any policies, processes, or directions contained within is the solitary and utter responsibility of the recipient reader. Under no circumstances will any legal responsibility or blame be held against the publisher for reparation, damages, or monetary loss due to the information herein, either directly or indirectly.

Respective authors own all copyrights not held by the publisher.

The information herein is offered for informational purposes solely and is universal as such. The presentation of the information is without a contract or any guarantee assurance.

The trademarks used are without any consent, and the publication of the trademark is without permission or backing by the trademark owner. All trademarks and brands within this book are for clarifying purposes only and are owned by the book owners, not affiliated with this document.

Contents

ARDUINO FOR BEGINNERS

Arduino For

Beginners

Beginners guide on How To Learn Arduino Advanced
Methods and Strategies

By

Robert Campbell

Introduction

Every day, everyone makes use of technology. Most individuals delegate programming to experts because they believe electronics and coding are tough and complex; they may be enjoyable and interesting pursuits. Designers, artists, students, and hobbyists learn how to make objects that glow, move, and react to animals, people, plants, or the world, thanks to Arduino. Thousands of projects have utilized Arduino as the "brain" throughout the years, each more inventive than the previous. A global community of creators has rallied around this free source platform, transforming personal computing into personal fabrication and helping to a different era of participation, collaboration, and sharing. Arduino is a simple and open platform. You can make learning to use digital technologies easy and accessible if you start with that premise. Electronics and code have suddenly become artistic instruments that everyone can use, similar to paintbrushes and paint. This book takes you through the fundamentals in a hands-on manner, with creative projects that you create as you learn. Once you've learned the fundamentals, you'll be able to employ various circuits and software to construct something beautiful and make someone happy with your invention.

This book will teach you about the Arduino programming language, its applications, and how it works.

- The Arduino Board's Description

- Installation of an Arduino

- The Arduino Program's Structure

- Arduino's Data Types

- Arduino Variables & Constants

- Programmers for Arduino

- Arduino Control Statements

- Arduino's Loops

- Arduino's Advantages

- Arduino's Strings

- Arduino String Object

- Arduino's Arrays

Chapter-1 Arduino Overview

Arduino Uno is an open electronics platform that uses simple hardware and software to make it easy to use. Arduino boards can take inputs - such as light from any finger on a button, a sensor, a social media message - and convert them to outputs - such as switching on an LED, triggering a motor, or posting anything online. By providing a sequence of commands to the board's microcontroller. The Arduino software program (centered on wiring), as well as the Arduino Interface (IDE) (based on Processing), are used to do this.

Thousands of projects have used Arduino throughout the years, ranging from simple household items to complicated scientific apparatus. This open-source platform has united an international society of makers - students, programmers, artists, amateurs, and professionals - whose contributions have added to an enormous quantity of accessible information that may greatly benefit beginners and specialists alike.

Arduino was created at the "Ivrea Interaction Design Institute" as a simple tool for rapid prototyping intended for students with no previous experience with electronics or programming. As soon as it gained a larger following, the Arduino board began to evolve to meet new requirements and problems, evolving from basic 8-bit boards to solutions for IoT, 3D printing, wearables, and embedded settings.

1.1 Why Arduino?

Arduino has been utilized in millions of projects and applications because of its convenient user interface. Beginners will find the Arduino software simple to use, while expert users will find it adaptable. It's compatible with Windows, Mac, and Linux. Teachers' other professionals use it and students to create low-cost scientific equipment, demonstrate chemistry and physics concepts, and begin learning programming and robotics. Architects and designers create interactive prototypes, while musicians and artists utilize them to create installations and try new instruments. Makers, for example, utilize it to construct many of the items on display at the Maker Faire. Arduino is a valuable tool for learning new skills. Anyone - youngsters, amateurs, artists, programmers - may get started experimenting by studying the step-by-step instructions

For physical computing, there are a variety of additional microprocessors and microprocessor platforms to choose from. Similar functionality may be found in Parallax Basic Stamp, Phi-gets, Net-0media's BX-24, MIT's Handy-board, and many more programs. All of these programs condense the complicated elements of microcontroller programming into an easy-to-use package. Although Arduino simplifies designing with microcontrollers, it has several advantages over other instructors, students, and curious enthusiasts.

1.2 Types of Arduino Boards

Arduino is a fantastic platform for developing ideas and innovations, but choosing the proper board may be difficult. If you're new to Arduino, you may have assumed that there's just one "Arduino" board, and that was it. In truth, there are several versions of the genuine Arduino boards and hundreds of clones from rivals. But don't worry; later in this chapter, you will learn which one to start with. The following are some examples of the many kinds of Arduino boards available. The authentic Arduino boards are those with the Arduino logo on them, although there are many excellent clones on the marketplace. One of the main reasons to purchase a clone is that they are usually less costly than the original. For example, Spark Fun and Adafruit provide Arduino boards less expensive but have the same quality as the originals. One word of caution, be cautious when purchasing boards from unknown vendors.

Another thing to think about when picking a board is indeed the sort of project you want to accomplish. If you want to make a wearable electrical project, the Lilypad boards from Spark fun are a good option. The Lilypad is intended to be sewed into wearable and e-textiles crafts with ease. If your work has a compact form factor, the Arduino Pro Mini, which has a very tiny footprint comparing to other boards, can be a good choice. For analysis and analysis of the top boards available, see Spark fun's Arduino Comparison Guide. Following that, you'll look at our preferred Arduino board, which is suggested novices begin with.

Arduino Uno

The Arduino Uno is among the most famous Arduino boards. Even though it was not the first board to be launched, it is still the most popular and well-documented on the market. Because of its widespread usage, the Arduino Uno has many projects and forums available on the Internet to assist you in getting started or getting out of a bind. Because of its amazing features and simplicity of use, you love the Uno.

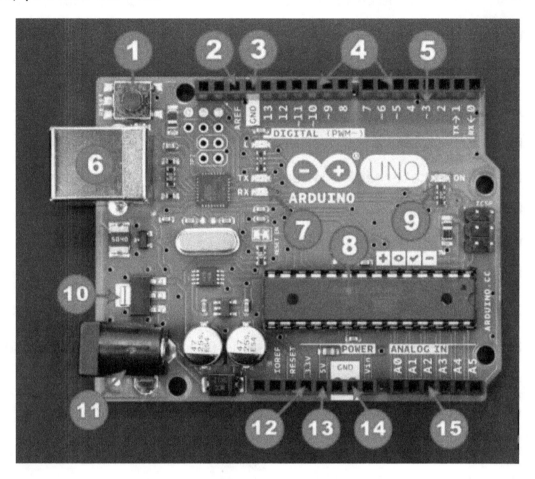

Breakdown of the Board

The components that comprise an Arduino UNO board are listed below, along with their functionalities.

- **Reset Button.** Pressing this button will reload any programming on the Arduino board.

- **AREF**. This acronym stands for "Analog Reference," which establishes an outside reference voltage.

- **Ground Pin**. The Arduino has many ground pins, all of which function in the same way.

- **PWM.** The pins indicated with the () symbol may emulate analog output.

- **USB Cable.** Used to power up the Arduino and upload programs.

- **TX/RX.** LEDs that indicate data transmission and reception.

- **AT Mega Microchip.** It is the brain of the board, which is where the programs are kept.

- **Power Indicator Light**. When the board is hooked into a power source, this LED illuminates.

- **Voltage Regulator.** It regulates the voltage supplied to an Arduino board.

- **3.3 volts Pin.** The Pin offers 3.3 hours of electricity to your work.

- **Dc Voltage Barrel Jack.** This Pin is used to power the Arduino with such a power source.

- **V Pin**. This Pin provides your projects with 5 volts of electricity.

- **Ground Pins.** The Arduino has several ground pins that all function the same way.

- **Analog Pins**. The pins can read analog sensor signals and transform them too digital.

Arduino Power Supply

The Arduino Uno requires a power supply to function and may be charged in several ways. You may connect the boards directly to your desktop using a USB connection, as most users do. Consider utilizing a 9V rechargeable battery to power your project if you want it to be portable. The last option is to utilize a 9V AC source of power.

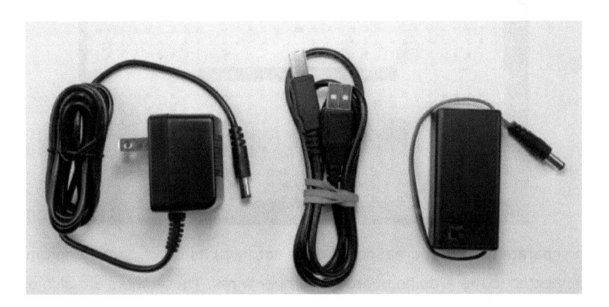

Arduino Breadboard

When working with Arduino, a solderless breadboard is also essential. You may use this gadget to develop your Arduino work without having to connect the circuit permanently. You may make additional prototypes and test with alternative circuit designs using a breadboard. Metal clips are joined via a strip of conductive material within the plastic housing slots (tie points).

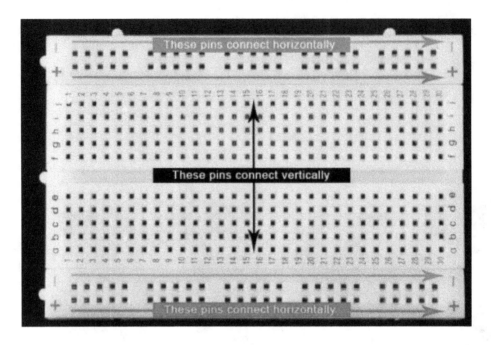

On a separate note, the breadboard does not have its power supply and must be connected to the Arduino board via jumper wires. These fibers are also used to link resistors, switches, and other elements to make the circuit.

1.3 Setting the Arduino Board

After you have studied the introduction of the Arduino and learned a bit about what You're programming, you'll learn how to install the software. You should turn on your computer and get started writing code. Getting Started When you purchase an Arduino board, it normally comes preloaded with an example Blink software that flashes the built-in light-emitting diode (LED). The LED is connected to one of the board's digital input-output ports. Digital pin 13 is linked to it. As a result, pin 13 can only be utilized as an output. However, since the LED only consumes a modest amount of electricity, you may still utilize that connection for other purposes. Using your Arduino start-up, all you have to do is connect it to a power source. The simplest method is to connect it to your computer's USB connection. You'll need a USB cable that converts from type A to type B. It's the same sort of cable that connects your computer to your printer. The LED should flash if everything is operating properly. This Blink sketch is pre-installed on new Arduino boards to ensure that the board is functional.

1.4 Installing the Software

You must do more than just give electricity to the Arduino board through USB to be required to activate fresh sketches. You should then upload a program to the Arduino board after successfully installing the Arduino board and, according to your system, USB drivers.

Putting Your First Sketch Online, the flashing LED is Arduino's version of the "Hello World" program, which is the usual first program to execute while learning a new language in other languages. Let's put the environment to the test by installing and changing this application on your Arduino board. When you first launch the Arduino computer, it displays an empty sketch.

Fortunately, the program comes with a large number of examples to get you started. So that's where the file menu comes in.

You must now upload or copy the sketch on your Arduino Uno board. So, using the USB cable, connect your Arduino board to your computer. The green LED on the Arduino should light up. An Arduino board will likely be blinking already since the Blink code is usually pre-installed on the boards. But first, let's reinstall it and then tweak it. If you're using a Macintosh, you could receive the notice "A network connection has been discovered" when you connect the board in. Simply click Cancel; the Mac is perplexed and believes the Arduino is a USB cable. You must inform the Arduino program what sort of board you use and whose serial port it connects to until you can load a sketch.

The serial port on a Windows computer is always COM3. On Linux or Macs PCs, the list of available serial devices is substantially larger). The device will usually appear at the top of the list, with a name that sounds like "/dev/tty.usbmodem621". Now, on the toolbar, click the Upload icon. There is a little wait when you hit the button while the drawing is constructed before the transmission starts. If it's functioning, you should see a flurry of LED flashing while the sketch is transmitted, followed by the message "Done Uploading" at the foot of the Arduino program window and another message that says something like "Binary sketch size: 1018 bytes" (Maximum 14336 byte).

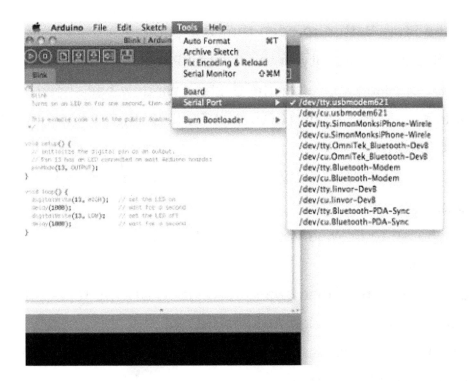

1.5 Arduino drivers

Arduino drivers must be installed. A USB port is available on Arduino boards. Before connecting the board to your computer through USB, you must first install appropriate drivers on the latter. There is a significant difference between OSX and Windows in this regard; OS X, for example, does not need any particular drivers for the Arduino Uno or the Mega 2560. If you're using an older board, you'll need to go to the FTDI website and download the current version of drivers, double-click the package, follow the instructions, and then restart your computer. You will study How it works with Windows computers, namely Windows 8,10 etc. Installing Arduino Uno R3 drivers to utilize the Arduino R3 and several other boards, you must first complete the procedures listed below. For the most up-to-date information, go to the Arduino website.

- Connect your board to the computer, then wait for Windows to complete the driver installation. The procedure eventually fails after a few seconds.

- Click the Start Button to open the control panel.

- Go to System & Security in the Control Panel. Then choose the system. Open Device Manager after the System window has shown.

- Look in the Ports section (COM & LPT). Examine the Arduino UNO open port (COMxx).

- Select Update Driver Software from the context menu of the Arduino UNO port.

- Next, choose to Browse your system for driver software from the drop-down menu.

- Finally, in the Arduino software download's Drivers folder, find and pick the Uno's driver file, titled ArduinoUNO.inf

- From there, Windows will complete the driver installation, and everything will be great.

1.6 C Language Basics

C is the programming language that is used to program Arduinos. You will learn the fundamentals of the C programming language. As an Arduino programmer, you'll use everything you've learned here to every sketch you create. These foundations are required to get the most out of Arduino.

People who speak other languages are not rare. In fact, and you study, the simpler it seems to be to acquire spoken languages, as you begin to see similar grammatical and lexical patterns. Programming languages are no exception. If you've ever used another programming language, you'll be able to take up C fast. The good news is that a programming language's vocabulary is far below that of a speaking language, but since you write it instead of speaking it, you can always check things up in the dictionary.

Furthermore, a programming language's grammar and syntax are remarkably consistent, and once you grasp a few basic principles, learning faster becomes second nature. An instruction—or a sketch, as the Arduino program is known—is best thought of as a series of instructions to be followed out in the order they are put down. Let's say you wanted to write something like this: Each of these three lines will do something. Pin 13's output would be set to HIGH in the first line. It is the Pin on the Arduino board with an LED built-in. Thus, the LED would light up at this point. The second line would patiently wait half a second before turning the LED off again, and the third line would do the same. As a result, these three lines will cause the LED to blink once. You've previously seen a surprising diversity of punctuation employed in unusual ways, as well as words with no spaces between them. "You know what You'd like to accomplish, but You don't know everything You need to write!" is a common dissatisfaction among inexperienced programmers. Don't worry, everything will be explained. First, let's take a look at the punctuation and how the words are created. Both of these elements are part of the language's syntax. Most languages demand exceptional precision in syntax, and one of the most important criteria is that object names must be one word. That is, they are unable to incorporate any spaces. So, digitalWrite is a brand name for a product. It's the name of a constructed function on the Arduino board that will set an output pin (you'll learn something about functions later). Names must not only be free of spaces, but they must also be case-sensitive. As a result, you must type digitalWrite rather than DigitalWrite or Digitalwrite. The function digitalWrite requires information about which port to set and whether that Pin should be set HIGH or LOW. These two data bits are referred to as arguments, and they are supplied to a function once it is called. A function's arguments must be separated by commas and surrounded in parentheses. The starting parenthesis should be placed directly after the final letter of the function's name, and space should be placed after the comma until the next argument. You may, however, use space characters inside the parenthesis if desired. There is no need for a comma if the function has only one parameter. Take note of the semicolon at the end of each line. Because the semicolon signals the conclusion of one instruction, similar to the conclusion of a sentence, it would have been more logical if they had been periods. You'll learn more about what occurs when you hit the Upload button also on the Arduino development environment in the following section (IDE).

1.7 Program writing for Arduino board

The Arduino Programming Language is a language that Arduino supports natively.

This program is based upon on Wiring development environment, which is based on Processing; it's what p5.js gets based on if you're unfamiliar with it. It has a rich history of projects growing on top of one other in an Open-Source manner. The Arduino IDE is primarily based on Processing IDE, which is based on the Wiring IDE.

When working with Arduino, you'll most likely use the Arduino Board Integrated Development Environment (IDE), a piece of software available for all major desktop environment (macOS, Windows, Linux) that provides us with two things: a programming editor with built-in libraries, and a way to quickly Load and compile our Arduino program onto a computer-connected board.

The Arduino Language is essentially a C++-based framework. You may argue that it isn't a true language of programming in the classic sense, but this helps newcomers avoid misunderstandings.

The sketch is the name for a program created in the Arduino Uno Programming Language. Normally, a drawing is stored with the ".ino" extension (from Arduino).

The key difference between it and "normal" C++ or C is that all of your code is wrapped into two primary functions. Of course, you may have more than two, but each Arduino program must have at least those two.

The first is known as setup (), and the second is known as a loop (). One is called first when your program begins, and the second is called "frequently" while running.

You don't have a main () function as you have in C/C++ as the program's entry point. When you compile your sketch, your IDE checks to see whether the final result is a valid C++ program and preprocesses it to add the missing glue.

Everything else is standard C++ code, and since C++ is a generalized form of C, any legitimate C code will work with Arduino.

One distinction that may create confusion is that, although you may launch your application over numerous files, they must also be in the folder. If your software becomes extremely big, this constraint may be a deal-breaker; however, at that time, it will be simple to switch to a local C++ arrangement, which is conceivable.

Built-in libraries are part of an Arduino Programming Language and enable you to quickly connect with the Arduino board's capabilities.

Your first Arduino program will almost certainly include turning on and off a light. You'll utilize the delay (), pinMode(), and digitalWrite() methods, as well as certain constants like LOW, HIGH, and OUTPUT, to do this.

1.8 Arduino sketch

You can probably identify an Arduino sketch and guess what it's attempting to accomplish, but you'll need to go a little further into how programming language code transforms from words on the page to something that can do anything, like turn an LED. "OFF" or "NO." This diagram depicts the whole process, from entering code into the Arduino IDE to executing the sketch on board.

When you hit the Upload button on the Arduino IDE, a series of actions occur, culminating in your sketch being installed and executed on the Arduino. It's not as simple as copying and pasting the text from the editor to an Arduino board. The first phase is a process known as compilation. It converts the code you've typed into machine code, which is the binary language that Arduino understands. When you use the Arduino IDE's triangle Verify button, it tries to compile the C code you've written instead of sending it all to the Arduino IDE. Compiling the code has the secondary benefit of ensuring that it plays by the rules of a C programming language.

Despite its Italian roots, the Arduino has attempted to assemble the words "Ciao Bella," but it has no clue what you're talking about. It is not a C text. Consequently, you get the puzzling warning "error: Ciao does not identify a type" at the edge of the screen. What this signifies is that there are several flaws in your writing.

Your attempts at creating code have been evaluated by the Arduino IDE and deemed to be acceptable. It informs you of this by announcing "Done Compiling" and providing you with the sketch's size: 450 bytes. The IDE also informs you that the maximum size equals 32,256 bytes, indicating that you have plenty of capacity to expand your drawing. Let's have a look at the source code that will serve as the foundation for every drawing you ever produce. There are a few new additions here. There's the term void, for example, as well as some curly brackets. Let's start with the emptiness.

You're creating a method named setup with the line void setup (). Some functions, such as delay and digitalWrite, are already specified for you in

Arduino, but you must or may create others. In every drawing you draw, you must specify two functions for yourself: setup and loop. The crucial thing to remember is that you are not using setup or loop in the same way that you would use digitalWrite; rather, you are constructing these functions so the Arduino system may call them. It is a tough notion to understand, but one thing to understand about it is as if you were reading a legal term.

Lawyers might make their papers shorter and more accessible by defining terms in the way—for example, using the word "author" as shorthand for "The person or individuals responsible for generating the book." Functions act in a similar way to definitions. You create a function that either you or your system may utilize in other parts of your drawings. Returning to void, as these two functions (loop and setup) may not return a value like some others, you must declare them void by using the void reserved words. If you imagine a function named sin that executed a trigonometric function of the same name, you'll see that it returns a value. The sin of an angle supplied as its parameter would be the value returned for using from the function. You construct functions using C that may then be called in C, similar to how a legal definition employs words to describe a term. The name of the function follows the special term void, followed by parentheses to hold any parameters. There are still no arguments in this situation, and the parenthesis must still be included. Because you are creating a function instead of calling it, there is no ";" semicolon after the ending parenthesis. You must state what will happen if the function is called.

Things that must happen when the function is invoked must be enclosed in curly brackets. A block of code is made up of curly brackets and the code that goes between them, and it's a notion you'll see again later. It's worth noting that you don't have to write any code in them though you must declare the functions loop and setup. Failure to include code, on the other hand, will make you're drawing a bit boring. Blink, Blink, Blink, Blink, Blink, Blink, B The setup and loop functions on Arduino are used to distinguish between tasks that must be completed just once, such as when the Arduino begins executing its sketch and tasks that must be completed repeatedly. When the sketch begins, the function setup will only be performed once. You should add additional code to it to make the LED on the board flash. After that, add the outlines to your sketch, look like this, and then publish it to your board.

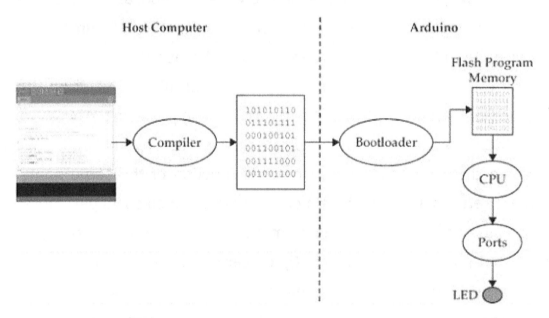

1.9 LCD Module with Arduino

Do you want to show status updates or sensor data on your Arduino projects? Then these LCD screens could be just what you're looking for. They're highly prevalent and a quick approach to give your product a legible interface.

You will learn everything you need to know about Character LCDs and how to use them. Not only 16 by 2(1602) but then any character Lcd screens (for example, 16 by 4, 16 by 1, 20 by 4, etc.) that use Hitachi's HD44780 parallel connection LCD controller chip. Because the Arduino team has already created a library for dealing with HD44780 LCDs, you'll be able to connect them in no time.

Liquid Crystal Display (LCD) is a display device that generates a visible picture using liquid crystals.

When current is sent through this unique kind of crystal, it becomes opaque, blocking the backlight from behind the screen. As a consequence, that specific region will seem darker than the others. That's how the characters appear on the screen.

1.10 Hardware Overview

The moniker "Character LCD" comes from the fact that LCDs are best for showing simply text or characters. The display features an LED backlight and can show 32 ASCII characters in 2 lines of 16, with each row displaying 16 characters.

You can see the small rectangles for every character on display, as well as the pixels that go up a character if you look carefully. Any one of these rectangles is a 588-pixel grid.

Although they show text, they are available in various sizes and colors, including 16 by 1, 16 by 4, 20 by 4, white color on a blue backdrop, black text on green, and many more.

The great news is that some of these screens are 'swappable,' meaning that if you create your project with one, you can simply unplug it and replace it with a different size/color LCD. Your code may need to change to accommodate the increased size, but the wiring remains the same! Let's have a look at the LCD Pinout before You go into the connections and sample code.

GND should be linked to Arduino's ground is the LCD's power source, which you connect to the Arduino's 5 volts pin. The LCD contrast and brightness are controlled by Vo (LCD Contrast). You may fine-tune the contrast by using a simple voltage divider and a potentiometer.

The RS (Register Select) pin tells the Arduino whether it's delivering instructions or data to the LCD. This Pin is mostly used to distinguish instructions from data.

When the RS pin is set at LOW, for example, you send orders to the LCD. When the RS pin is set to HIGH, data/characters are sent to the LCD.

The read/Write Pin upon on LCD is used to regulate whether you're reading and writing data to a display. You'll tie this pin LOW since you'll only be utilizing the LCD as just an OUTPUT device. It switches it to WRITE mode.

The display is turned on using the E (Enable) pin. When this Pin is set at LOW, the LCD is unconcerned with what is going on with the R/W, RS, and data bus lines; when it is set to HIGH, the LCD is analyzing the incoming data.

1.11 Testing Character LCD

You've arrived at the exciting part. Let's put your LCD to the test. Connect the Arduino Uno's 5V and GND pins to the board power rails, then plug your LCD into the breadboard. You'll now turn on the LCD. The LCD has two independent power connections: one for the LCD itself (Pin 1 and Pin 2), another for the LCD backlight (Pin 15 and Pin 16). Connect the LCD's pins 1 & 16 to GND and ports 2 and 15 to 5V.

Chapter 2: Arduino C

With the founding of the X3J11 commission in 1983, the C language started its journey to become legally standardized by the American National Standard Institute (ANSI). In 1989, the committee's work was done, and the standard was approved. Ever since the language has been dubbed "ANSI C." The ISO (International Organization for Standardization) has also accepted the standard. Hence, it is frequently referred to as "ISO C." ANSI C are the same. Both versions are also referred to as "standard C" in a culture obsessed with political correctness.

The C you're going to learn isn't your typical C. Instead, you'll learn a solid subset of conventional C. There are a few C features that aren't present. However, the lack of such qualities is by no means a fatal blow. You'll quickly realize that the Arduino C subset of normal C is more than capable of handling just about any job you could throw at it. The lack of features may readily be compensated for, though in a less attractive way.

2.1 Building Blocks

From Ada to ZPL, all programming languages are made up of four essential elements:

- Expression:
- Statements
- Blocks of statements
- Function Blocks

The fourth portion, function blocks, is known by a variety of names in a different language, including "methods" in Java, C++ "procedures" in Pascal, "subroutines" in Basic or Fortran, and potentially a more obscure title in lesser-known languages. Function blocks, regardless of their name, are code blocks that perform a certain task. Programs are just a collection of these elements that have been structured in a way that solves issues.

Expression:

Pairing operands and operators yield an expression. An operand, simply put, is a set of data that is operated on with an operator. A logical or mathematical action performed on one or more operands is known as an operator.

Examples of expressions are x + y, a –12 r> you. In the first case, the operands x and y are joined together in a math operation using the + operator. The numerical constant 12 (an operand) is subtracted (a – operator) from the operand labeled an in the second example. Operand r is compared to operand d in the previous example to see whether u is smaller than (the operator) d. Rather than a math operator, the relational operator (e.g., the "less than" operator, or) is used in the final example. The two operands are combined with the single operator to generate an expression in all three instances. An addition expression is the first, a subtraction expression is the second, and a relationship expression is the third.

There are two operands and one operator in these expressions. As a result, such expressions are often referred to as binary operator expressions. Binary operators (for example, +, –, and) always have two operands. Another thing to remember is that every expression will resolve to a value at some point. (Some unary operators only need one operand, and ternary operators need three.) The binary operators, on the other hand, are the most popular in C.

Expressions may be mixed and matched. Consider the following scenario: x = 1, y = 2, and z = 3. A complicated expression may be written as x+y +z.

Because all equations have a value, you may solve the first one, x +y, which can be simplified to 11 + 12 + z.

Because the first phrase is now entirely of integers, it may be resolved to the value 3.

The complicated phrase may then be reduced to 3 + z

Take note of what occurred here. You resolved one of the expressions (i.e., x + y) into three from a complicated expression containing two operators and three operands. However, you simplified the complicated expression to a simple expression, 3 + C, in the process. The remaining equation may now be written as

3 + C.

3+3 =6

The complicated expression with two subexpressions is now resolved to a single value, 6, and the complicated expression with two sub-expressions is now resolved to a single value, 6. This process of reducing a complicated expression is sometimes referred to as factoring or resolving an expression.

How about g< d, a relational expression? If r= 15 and u = 14, the equation is: r<u false

Because 15 is larger than 14, not less than 14, the expression evaluates too false.

"Wait a minute!" you could exclaim. All expressions you just mentioned evaluates to a value. "False" is a word, not a value." True. However, logic false and logic true expressions in programming languages do resolve to a value. Logic true evaluates to a non-zero number (e.g., −1) in most languages, whereas logic false resolves to zero.

Because relational expressions are built to evaluates to a logic False or true state, they will eventually resolve to a value that can be utilized in a program.

Statement

A statement is indeed a full computer C instruction. A semicolon is used after every C statement (;). Here is some example of C statements:

s= 50;

x = y + z;

a = b / 2;

The assignment operator (=) is used to "assign" the value on the right side of the equation to the operand upon the equal sign's left side in the first example.

As a result, variable s is given the value 50 in the first sentence. Note that the first statement is nothing more than an assignment operator expression with a semicolon at the end of the line. 50 and variable s are the operands. A variable is nothing other than a memory region that has been given a name.

You have a complicated phrase with such a semicolon at the end of the second sentence. Because the result to assign to variable an is unknown in this example, you must first resolve the phrase x + y to get a value. If x = 14 and z=15, the complicated statement may be reduced to x = y + z x = 14+15 x = 29

Variable an is assigned the value 29 in the final phrase. By adding a semicolon at the end of the statement, the expression is transformed into a statement that changes the value of variable a to 29. On the other hand, the semicolon causes the C compiler to complete whatever work the statement requires. If you have a complicated statement like x = y+ z −c+h+j+m, the compiler must first resolve all intermediate expressions (a+b,c+g,h k) before determining what new value to assign x.

Statement Blocks

A statement block is made up of one or even more statements that have been grouped such that the compiler treats them as if they were a single statement. Assume you're apartment management, and there's 3 inches or more of snow; you'll need to shovel the walkway. You might write it like this (the >= operator means "greater than or equal to "):

```
if (snow>=3) {
Put_On_Snow_Removal_Stuff();
Get_Snow_Shovel();
Shovel_Side_walk();
} else {
Go_Back_To_Bed();
}
```

An initial brace character "{" precedes a statement block, which is followed by a closing brace character. A statement block body is made up of all statements between both the open or closed braces. In our example, You seem to put on your coats, get a shovel, and snow shovel the sidewalks when there are three or more inches of snow. A separate statement block is run. There is smaller than 3 inches of snow (i.e., You go back to bed). Within the statement block, you may put whatever form of statement you want. In the following chapters, you'll see a number more instances of this. Consider a statement block to be defined by opening and closing braces for the time being.

Function Blocks

The function block would be a snippet of code that performs a single function. You utilized the function block throughout the preceding section, even though you weren't aware of it. Put_On_Snow_Removal_Stuff(), in other words, is a method that instructs you to put on your coat. The real code may look something like this:

```
void_Put_On_Snow_Removal_Stuff(void) {
if (Not_Dressed) {
 Put_On_Clothes();
 Put_On_Shoes();
}
Go_To_Closet();
Put_On_Boots();
Put_On_Coat();
Put_On_Gloves();
Put_On_Hat();
}
```

The function block in this example similarly begins with an initial brace and finishes with a closing brace. On the other hand, function blocks are often created to create "black boxes," The specifics of how You accomplish anything are hidden inside the function. You may be considering building the code for a robot that will need sensors to detect what is ahead. You may create a TurnRight() method that causes your robot to turn 90° to the right. It most likely entails rotating one of the wheels, maybe by increasing the voltage applied to a stepper motor, causing the front wheels to move to the right. However, you may elect to modify your robot's wheels from four to three at a later time. You no longer need to spin two wheels; just one is required. Because the intricacies of turning your robots to the right are hidden in the Turn Right () black box, you have only to alter the program code in one place rather than a variety of locations where a right turn could be required. You may avoid repeating all of the TurnRight() method instructions on each occasion a right turn is required in the application by developing a TurnRight() function.

Another illustration could be useful. Assume you're creating an application that takes a phone number from a keypad and enters it into a database. Home, mobile, and work phone numbers are required for your application. To ensure that a legitimate phone number was input, make sure it follows the "1-000-000-0000" format. You could neither construct a Check_Phone_Format() method and call it three times, or you could replicate the format checking program code three times throughout the application. Let's have a look... Create the code three times, test it, debug it, or write a function once and debug it. To me, it seems to be a no-brainer. Additionally, by avoiding repeating the code, you will use fewer memory resources while calling functions.

If you consider a computer program as a series of smaller activities, you'll see that function blocks are utilized to separate the code for each one of them. The Arduino programming language offers hundreds, if not hundreds, of pre-written function blocks, which you may utilize in your applications, as you will soon discover. It implies you won't have to innovate every time you encounter a typical programming job.

You copy and paste an existing function block from the library of pre-written function blocks into your software. Since you can walk on the shoulders of developers who have already committed to a C++ library that you can use, life is nice and frequently simpler!

Every program you can imagine is made up of the four fundamental components covered in the section. Indeed, the remainder of the book is devoted to demonstrating how to utilize these basic components to solve a specific programming issue. However, therein is the issue. There are endless ways to put these pieces together in a computer program, some of which will function and others that will not. Just because your software works doesn't imply, there isn't a better (or more efficient?) method to do the same goal. Consider the following scenario: you would like to sort a collection of numbers into a list from the least to the greatest number inside the group. There are several methods for sorting a list of integers into ascending order, each with its own set of benefits and drawbacks. In fact, as your study something about programming in general, you'll discover that your options expand. Even basic tasks like scanning a series of text for a certain pattern may be accomplished in various methods. More the programming knowledge and expertise you gather, the more elegant solutions to programming problems you will be able to create. After all, if your primary instrument is a hammer, it's not a surprise that all of your issues resemble nails.

Furthermore, as the difficulty of a job grows, so does the number of possible solutions. If someone asked you to create fire alarms for a hotel, you'd probably come up with a million different ideas.

2.2 The Five-step C Arduino programing

Every program you can conceive of can be broken down into five fundamental phases or parts. When you're initially starting to build a program, think about it in terms of the Five Program Steps listed below.

Initialization Step

The Initialization Step's objective is to set up the environment where the application will execute. If you've used word or other comparable applications, you'll notice that the File command typically displays a list of the most frequently used files. You may set a home page in most web browsers. A default printer is typically included with a print application. A database software often establishes a preset network connection. Data is collected from someplace (e.g., a data file, RAM, EEPROM, or the registry) in each of these circumstances and utilized to create a basic environment where the program will execute.

Simply said, the Initialization Step performs any necessary background preparations before the program may begin executing to do its core job.

Input Step

Almost every computer program contains a job that takes a present condition of information, processes it somehow, and displays the new state of such information. If you're creating a fire suppression system, you'll take the data supplied by the flame sensors, assess their present status, and take action if there's a fire. If the sensor does not detect a fire, the procedure may be repeated with a second range of nodes. Indeed, your software may do nothing for decades except take fresh data every few seconds and evaluate if any corrective action is required. Regrettably, the day may arrive when a fire occurs, and immediate action is required. Nonetheless, the whole process is dependent on the timely entry of new data from the sensors.

The Input Phase is the set of program statements required to get the data required to complete the job at hand.

Process Step

Continuing using our fire alarm software, after the sensors' input is received, some code should be responsible for identifying whether or not the sensors have detected a fire. In other words, to ascertain the present condition of the sensors, the voltage (i.e., temperature) should be input and afterward interpreted (e.g., the data processed). Perhaps the data entered inside a desktop application is the price & quantity of an item bought by a consumer. The Process Step can be in charge of calculating the final cost to the customer. It's worth noting that software may contain many Process Steps. For example, determining the sales tax payable on a transaction may be a procedure with our customer. The procedure of calculating the total cost of the transaction becomes an output to calculate the sales tax owed in this situation. Another method might use the sales and tax owed as inputs.

On the other hand, the Process Step is in charge of accepting several objects and processing them to produce a new collection of data in all circumstances.

Output Step

The final value is generally output on a display device when the Processing Element has completed its task. In our consumer sales scenario, You might now show the entire amount owed to us by the customer. The Output Step, on the other hand, isn't only about showing the new data. New data is often stored or passed along to another application. For instance, the software may collect sales data during the day and update data at night so that another software can prepare purchase orders for management to see the following morning. Under typical settings, the Output Step in the fire alarm instance may cause an LED for a specific sensor to show a green hue. If a fire occurs, the LED may turn red, allowing those in charge to see which part of the structure is on fire.

The Output Phase is in charge of putting the Process Step's results to good use. This application might be as simple as showing the current information on a monitor screen or transferring the new value to another software.

Termination Step

After the program has completed its mission, the Termination Step is responsible for "cleaning up." In a desktop program, the Termination Step often performs the Initialization Step "backward." In that instance, if the program maintains a list of the most recently utilized data files, the Termination Step should update that list. If the Initializing Step establishes a database and printer connection, the Termination Step must terminate that connection to free up system resources.

Many mc programs, on the other hand, are not intended to be terminated. As long as conditions are "normal," a fire alarm is likely to keep working indefinitely. Even then, there may be a Termination Process in place. For example, if a component throughout the fire alarm fails, the Session may attempt to locate the faulty component until the system is shut down for repairs. Before a maintenance shutdown, the Termination Process may disable the alarm system.

2.3 Arduino C Data Types

With a few significant exceptions, Arduino C supports the majority of ANSI C data types. There's also some hanky-panky with floating - point, but that shouldn't be an issue if you understand what's going on "under the hood."

A variable is nothing more than a slice of storage that was given a name. When you declare a variable, you must also specify the kind of data associated with it. The type of data of even a variable is significant because it dictates however many bytes of memory are allocated to it, and what types of data may be stored in it. There are two fundamental categories of data: values types and reference types, as you'll see later in this chapter. If the variable is declared as just a value type, a very narrow range of values is also conceivable.

2.4 Keywords in C

Any term that has particular significance to a C compiler is referred to as a keyword. You can't utilize keywords with your function or variable names since they're reserved for the compiler. When you do, a compiler may report you as having made a mistake. If the compiler did not flag such mistakes, it would be unsure which keywords to employ in any given case.

Chapter 3: Functions

This chapter focuses on the functions you can create instead of the built-in functions like delay and digitalWrite that are already specified for you. You should develop your functions because as your drawings get more involved, your loop and setup routines will get longer and more sophisticated, making it harder to understand how they operate. The most difficult aspect of any software development project is dealing with complexity. The finest programmers create software that is simple to look at and comprehend, with little explanation required. Functions are an important tool for producing simple, easy-to-understand drawings that may be altered without difficulty or the danger of the whole document collapsing. What is the definition of a function? A function is similar to a program inside a program in that it is a program inside a program. It may be used to do any little task you have. A defined function may be called anywhere in the sketch and has its own set of variables and directives. After the instructions have been executed, execution resumes where it left off in the program that invoked the function. For instance, code that flashes the LED (light-emitting diode) is an excellent example of code that belongs in a function. So, let's update our simple "blink 20 times" sketch to include a method you'll name flash:

So, all you've done is relocate the four pieces of text that flash the LED from the "for-loop" midsection to a flash function. You now can create the LED flash whenever you want by just putting flash to the new function (). After the function name, notice the empty parenthesis. It means that the function has no input arguments. The delay value is determined by the delay period function, which you used before. Variables When breaking your drawing into functions, it's helpful to consider what kind of service each function may give. It is quite clear in the instance of flash. But this time, let's give this function some arguments that tell it how many repetitions to flash and how brief or long to flash. After you've gone through the code below, you will go through how parameters operate in more depth.

```
int ledPin = 13;
int delayPeriod = 250;

void setup()
{
  pinMode(ledPin, OUTPUT);
}

void loop()
{
  flash(20, delayPeriod);
  delay(3000);
}

void flash(int numFlashes, int d)
{
  for (int i = 0; i < numFlashes; i ++)
  {
    digitalWrite(ledPin, HIGH);
    delay(d);
    digitalWrite(ledPin, LOW);
    delay(d);
```

If you check the loop function now, you'll see that it just contains two lines. You've delegated the majority of the job to a flash function. Notice how you now provide two parameters in parentheses to flash when you call it. You must identify the type of variable in the arguments when you specify the function at the sketch base. They're both integers in this scenario. In reality, you're creating new variables.

On the other hand, the variables number Flashes may only be utilized inside the flash function. It is a useful function since it contains all of the information required to flash a LED. The only information it requires from outside the function is the Pinto to which the LED is connected. You could also make it a parameter if you wanted to, which would be useful if you could have more than one LED connected to your Arduino.

Functions enable you to break down the program into smaller chunks of code that accomplish specific functions. When you need to do the same action numerous times in a program, you should create a function.

Organizing code fragments in functions provides several benefits.

- Functions aid in the programmer's organization. It often helps in the conceptualization of the program.
- Functions codify one operation in one place, reducing the number of times a function must be thought about it and debugged, as well as the number of times the code must be modified.
- Because chunks of code are reused several times, functions make the entire sketch shorter and more compact.
- They make it simpler to reuse code in other programs by making it modular, and they make it more understandable by employing functions.

In an Arduino sketch or program, setup () and loop () are essential functions; further functions must be written outside the parentheses of these two procedures.

3.1 Function Declaration

A function is defined above or below the loop function, outside of any other functions.

There are two methods to define the function.

The first method is to simply write the component of the function known as a function prototypes just above loop function, which comprises the following:

- The return type of a function

- Function name

- Function argument type (the argument name does not need to be written)

A semicolon must follow the function prototype (;).

```
int sum_function(int a, int y) // "function declaration"

{

int c = 0;

c =a+b;

return c; // return the integer value

}

void setup ()

{Statements // set of statements

}


Void loop(){

int result = 0;

result = Sum_function (15,61); // "calling of a function"

}
```

The second portion, known as the function Declaration or definition, should be declared just after the loop function, which is made from:

- Function return type

- Function name

- Function argument type, where the argument name must be included

- The body's function (when function is calling the statements inside the function will execute)

The following example shows how to use the second technique to declare a function.

```
int sum_function (int,int ) ; // function_prototype
void setup(){
   Statements // sets of statements
}
void loop(){
   int result= 0;
   result = Sum_function(15,61); // function calling
}


int sum_func (int x, int y) // function declaration {
   int z = 0;
   z = x+y ;
   return z; // return the value
}
```

The second method just declares the function above the loop function.

3.2 Built-in Functions

In this part, you will give a reference for the Arduino Programming Language's built-in functions.

Program lifecycle

- Setup () is called once when the program begins and again when the Arduino gets turned off and on.
- While the Arduino program is running, the loop () function is called repeatedly.

3.3 Handling I/O

The following routines assist you in managing your Arduino device's input and output.

Digital Input/Output

- **Digital Read():** It reads a digital pin's value. Returns the Low or High constant when given a PIN as an input.

- **DigitalWrite():** It sets the value of a digital output signal pin to Low or high the PIN and HIGH or LOW, given as parameters.

- **PinMode():** It determines whether a pin is an input or an output. As arguments, you supply the PIN and the OUTPUT or INPUT value.

- **Pulse In():** It reads a digital pulse on a pin from High to Low and back to High, or from low to high and back to low. Until the pulse is detected, the program will halt. You choose the pin code and the kind of pulse to detect (HLH or LHL). To cease waiting for that pulse, you may provide an optional timeout.

- **PulseInLong():** It is the same as pulse in (), except that it is implemented uniquely and cannot be used whenever disabled. Interrupts are often disabled to get a more precise result.

- **Shifting():** It reads a piece of data from a pin one bit at a time.

- **Shift Out():** It writes one bit by bit to a pin a byte of data.

- **Tone():** It delivers a square wave on a pin used to play tones on buzzers and speakers. You may choose the Pin as well as the frequency. It is compatible with both digital and analog pins.

- On a pin, No Tone () disables the tone () produced wave.

Analog Input/Output

- **Analog Read ():** It reads an analog pin's value.
- **Analog Reference ():** It sets the value for the analog input's top input range by defaulting 5 volts on 5-volt boards and 3.3 volts on 3.3 volts boards.
- **Analog Write():** It is a function that writes an analog value to a pin.
- **AnalogReadResolution():** It modifies the default analog bit resolution for analog Read (),set to 10 bits by default. Only on certain devices does it operate (Arduino Zero, MKR and Due)
- **AnalogWriteResolution():** It modifies the default analog bits resolution for analog Write (),set to 10 bits by default. Only on certain devices does it operate (Arduino Zero, MKR and Due)

3.4 Time functions

- **delay()**: It stops the program for the supplied number of milliseconds. Postponement Microseconds () stops the application for a given number of microseconds.
- **Micros ():** It indicates the number of microseconds because the program began. Due to overload, it resets after 70 minutes.
- **Millis ():** It indicates the number of milliseconds because the program began. Due to overload, it resets after 50 days.

3.5 Math functions

- **abs()**: It returns a number's absolute value; restrict() limits a number's range; see use
- **map()**: It remaps several one ranges to another; for more information, see use.
- **Max ()**: It returns the sum of two numbers.
- **Min ():** It returns the smaller of two values.
- **Pow ()**: It returns the net present value multiplied by a power.
- **sq()** It returns the square of an integer; sqrt() returns the square root of an integer.
- **Cos ():** It returns the cosine of an angle given.
- **Sin ():** It returns the sine of an angle given.
- **Tan ()** It returns the tangent of an angle given.

3.6 characters functions

- **alphanumeric():** It determines if a char is an alpha (a letter) or alphanumeric (a number or letter)
- **Ascii()**: It determines if a char is an ASCII character
- **isControl()**: It determines if a char is a control character
- **isDigit():** It determines if a char is a number
- **isGraph()**: It determines whether a char is a printed ASCII character with content (not space, for example).
- **isHexadecimal():** It determines whether a char is a hexadecimal value.
- **isLowerCase():** It tests whether a character in lowercase letters (A to F 0 to 9) • Digit() tests whether a char is a hexadecimal digit (A to F 0 to 9).
- **isPrintable()**: It determines if a char is a printed ASCII character.
- **isPunct():** It determines if a character is a punctuation character (a semicolon, a comma, an exclamation mark etc.)

- **isSpace():** It determines if a character is a space, a form feed, a newline, a carriage return, a horizontal tab, or a vertical tab.
- **isUpperCase():** It determines if a character is an upper-case letter
- **isWhitespace():** It determines if a character is a space letter or a horizontal tab

3.7 Random numbers

- random(): It returns a pseudo-random number

- randomSeed(): It sets an arbitrary beginning value for the pseudo-random number generator.

It's hard to generate random numbers in Arduino, as it is in other languages, and the series is the same, so either seed it with the present time or (in the instance of Arduino) receive the input from such an analog port.

3.8 bits and bytes

- **bit():** It returns the bit value ("0 = 1", "1 = 2", "2 = 4", "3 = 8"...)
- **bitClear():** It clears a numeric variable (sets it to 0). Accepts a number as well as the bit number, beginning from the right.
- **bitRead():** It reads a single digit from an integer. Accepts a number as well as the bit number, beginning from the right.
- **bitSet():** It sets a bit of an integer to one. Accepts a number as well as the bit number, beginning from the right.
- **bitWrite():** It assigns a value one or Zero to a single bit of an integer. Accepts a number, a bit number beginning on the right, as well as the value to write (Zero or 1)
- **highByte(:)** It returns the word variable's high-order (leftmost) byte (which has 2 bytes)

- **lowByte():** It has the low-order (rightmost) byte of a word variable using (which has 2 bytes)

3.9: Interrupts

- **noInterrupts():** Interruptions are disabled when is used.

- **attachInterrupt():** It allows an input signals pin to be used as an interrupt after being deactivated by interrupts(). Check the official documents to see what pins are authorized on each board. It enables an interrupt; detachInterrupt() disables it ()

Chapter 4: Arrays and Strings

An array is a group of variables that may be retrieved by using an index number. Arrays may be sophisticated in the C++ that Arduino sketches are created in, but utilizing basic arrays is easy, and Strings are being used to store text. They may be used to show text through an LCD or in the Serial Monitor window of the Arduino IDE. Arrays of characters are the same as the characters used in C programming, are also handy for storing user input. The Arduino String is a program that allows us to utilize a string object.

4.1 Arrays

Arrays are a kind of data structure. Arrays are a kind of data structure that can hold a range of items. So far, all of the variables you've seen have only had one value, generally an int. On the other hand, an array has a range of items, and you may access any of them by their position in terms. C, like the majority of computer languages, starts indexing positions at 0 instead of 1. As a result, the first item is the zeroth element. To demonstrate the usage of arrays, construct an example program that allows the Arduino board's built-in LED to flash "SOS" in Morse code repeatedly. In the nineteenth and twentieth centuries, the Morse code was an important mode of communication. Morse code may be conveyed through telegraph lines, through a radio connection, or utilizing signaling lights since it encodes letters as a succession of short and long dots. The letters "SOS" (an abbreviation for "save our souls") are still used as a distress signal across the world. Three small lights (dots) depict the letter "S," whereas three extended flashes depict the letter "O." (dashes). To keep track of the length of each flash, you'll utilize an array of int. After that, you could use the for loop to walk over each item in the array, flashing for the proper amount of time. Let's start by looking at how you'll construct an array of int holding the durations. By adding [] after a variable's name, you may indicate that it includes an array. In this situation, the values and durations will be set when the array is created. Curly braces are used as a starting point, followed by values separated by commas. Remember to use a semicolon at the back of the line. The square bracket syntax may be used to access any member in the array. For example, if you wish to obtain the first element of an array, you may write: Let's establish an array and print out all of its contents to the Serial port to demonstrate this.

With arrays, you must be cautious since the compiler would not attempt to prevent you from accessing data beyond the array's end. The arrays are a reference to a memory location. Data, including conventional variables and arrays, are kept in memory by the program. Computer memory is far more strictly organized than human memory. It's easy to conceive of an Arduino's memory as a series of pigeonholes. When you create an array of nine items, for example, the next nine pigeon holes are set aside for it, as well as the variable is said to refer to the array's initial pigeonhole or element. Returning to our earlier point about accessing data outside of your array's limits, you would still get an int from memory if you wanted to read durations [10]. However, the value of this int might be anything.

4.2 Example Of an arrays

```
int array_name[ 10 ] ; //an array with ten variables

void setup()

{

}

void loop () {

    for (int a = 1; a <= 10; a++ )
```

```
{
    Array_name[a] = 1;
    Serial.print (a);
    Serial.print ('\r');
  }
  for ( int x = 1; x <= 10; ++x )
{
    Serial.print (array_name[x]);
    Serial.print ('\r');
  }
}
```

An equal-to(=) sign and a brace-delimited semicolon list of initializers may also be used to initialize the array elements in the array definition. An initializer list is used to create an integer array containing ten values (line a), then printed in a tabular fashion.

```
int array_name [10] ={ 132, 127, 164, 118, 195, 114, 190, 170, 160, 137 }
;
void setup(){
}
void loop(){
for ( int x =1; x < =10; ++x ) {
Serial.print (x);
Serial.print('\r') ;
```

```
}
for ( int a =1; a<=10; ++a ){
Serial.print (array_name[a]) ;
Serial.print ('\r') ;
}
}
```

Arrays are crucial to Arduino and therefore should be given greater consideration. An Arduino programmer should understand the following key array ideas.

Arrays Passed to Functions

To send an array parameter to a function, just type the array's name without the brackets.

Arrays (Multi-Dimensional)

Arrays having two dimensions (i.e., subscripts) are often used to depict tables of values with rows and columns of data.

4.3 String

Text is stored using strings. They may be used to show text over an LCD or in the Serial Monitor window of the Arduino IDE. Strings may also be used to store user input. For instance, the characters which a user writes on an Arduino-connected keypad.

In Arduino programming, there are two sorts of strings:

- Arrays of characters that are the same as strings in C programming.
- The Arduino String object, which allows us to utilize a text string in our sketches.

4.4 Character Arrays

The first sort of string you'll study is a string that consists of a sequence of char characters. You learned what an array, a sequence of the same kind of data stored in memory. A string is a collection of character variables.

A string is a specialized array with an important addition at the end of a string that is always set to 0. (zero). A zero at the end is known as "null terminated string"

Example

```
void setup(){
Char my_string [7];
Serial.Begin(9600);
my_string[0] = 'A';
my_string[1] = 'b';
my_string [2] = 'c';
my_string [3] = 'd';
my_string [4] = 'e';
my_string [5] = 0; // "null terminator"
Serial.println(my_string);
}
void loop(){
}
```

The following example demonstrates a string composed of a character array containing printable characters with 0 as the array's final member to indicate that the string terminates here. Utilizing Serial. println() and giving the string's name, the string may be printed to an IDE of Arduino Serial Monitor window.

```
void setup(){

char my_string [] = "Coding";

Serial.begin(9600);

Serial.println(my_string);

}

void loop ()

{

}
```

4.5 Manipulating String Arrays

As seen in the following sketch, you may change a string array inside a drawing.

```
void setup(){

char love [] = " You love Coding";

Serial.begin(9600); // (1) printing the string

Serial.println(love); // (2) deleting the string

love[2] = 0;

Serial.println(love);    //(3) substitute string

love [13] = ' ';

love[18] = 'b'; // insert the new word

love[19] = "o";
```

```
love[20] = 'o';

love[21] = k;

Serial.println(love);

}

void loop() {

}
```

Result

You love coding

You Love

4.6 reducing the length of the string

By changing the 14th letter inside the string("I like cake and coffee") with a "null" means ending zero, the length is shortened (2). It is the thirteenth entry in the string array, counting from zero. All characters in the string are written up to a new null ending zero when it is printed. The remaining characters do not vanish; they remain in memory, or the string array remains the same size. The only distinction is that any string-related function will only view the string until it reaches a first null terminator.

4.7 Exchange of "Words."

Finally, the term "cake" is replaced with "tea" in the drawing (3). It must first substitute the "null terminator" at example[12] with such a space to return the string to its original format. New characters replace the letter "cak" in the term "cake" with the letter "tea." Individual characters are overwritten to do this. A new null ending character replaces the "e" in "cake." Consequently, the string is ended with two "null characters," one at the end of a string and the other replacing the "e" in "cake." When the new string is written, this makes no impact since the string characters' function terminates when it meets the first "null terminator."

```
void setup(){
char example[] = "I like cake and coffee";
Serial.begin(9600);
Serial.println(example);
example[12] = 0;
Serial.println(example);


  like[12] = ' ';
  like[13] = 'd'; // new word
  like[14] = 'i';
  like[15] = 'n';
  like[16] = 0; // terminate the string
  Serial.println(example);
}
void loop() {
}
```

Result

I like cake and coffee

I like cake

I like coffee and din

4.8 Length of an Array

The size of the array, which includes the string, is obtained using the operation size of (). The length contains the null terminator; therefore, it is one longer than the string's length. Size of () seems to be a function, but it is an operator. It is not part of the C strings library, but it was used during the sketch to demonstrate the difference between array and string sizes (or string length).

4.9 Copy of an array

To copy my string [] string to your string[] array, use the strcpy () function. The strcpy () method replaces the initial string with the second string provided to it. You still have 23 free char parts in the array since a duplicate of the string exists in your string[] array, but it only takes up 19 of the array's 18 members. These free items are found in memory following the string.

The string was transferred to the array so that there would be enough room in the array for the following portion of the sketch, which is attaching a string to the end of the string.

To a String, append a String (Concatenate). Concatenation is the process of joining two strings together in the drawing. "The strcat ()" function is used to do this. The strcat () method appends the second string it receives to end the first text it receives. The length is displayed after concatenation to illustrate the format string length. The array's length is then reported, indicating that you have a 26-character string in a 40-element array; because of the null ending zero, a 25-character long string occupies 26 characters of an array.

```
void setup(){
char my_string[] = "First string is mine";
char your_string [40];
```

```
int nu;

Serial.begin(9600);

Serial.println(str);

nu = strlen(str);

Serial.print("String length is: ");

Serial.println(num);

nu= sizeof(str);

Serial.print("Size of the array: ");

 Serial.println(nu);

strcpy(your_string, str);

Serial.println(your_string);

strcat(your_string, " sketch.");

Serial.println(your_string);

nu= strlen(your_string);

Serial.print("String length is: ");

Serial.println(nu);

  nu= sizeof(your_string);

  Serial.print("Size of your_string []: ");

 Serial.println(nu);
}

void loop(){

}
```

4.10 Array Bounds

When dealing with strings & arrays, staying inside the constraints of the strings or arrays is critical. In the sample sketch, a 40-character array was built to allocate memory that can be used to edit strings.

If you attempted to copy the string larger than the array because the array was too tiny, the string would've been copied so over the end of the array. Other critical data utilized in the sketch may be stored in the memory further than the end of the array, which the string would overwrite. Unless the memory far beyond the end of a string is exceeded, the sketch may crash or behave unexpectedly.

Chapter 5 The Standard Arduino Library

There are several additional libraries and operating systems for various types of devices available. These drivers may be found on sites such as Github, Arduino Playground and CGoogle Code.

User-installed libraries should be placed into your sketchbook library folder so that they may be used with any IDE version. You won't have had to reinstall all of your favorite libraries whenever the latest version of an IDE is released!

5.1 Data storage

An Arduino sketch is saved in flash memory (program space). When the sketch runs, it generates and manipulates variables in SRAM; EEPROM is a kind of memory that programmers may utilize to save long-term data.

The microcontroller used in Arduino boards has three memory pools:

- An Arduino sketch is saved in flash memory (program space).
- When the sketch runs, it generates and manipulates variables in SRAM
- An EEPROM is a kind of memory that programmers may utilize to store long-term data.

A non-volatile memory such as flash memory and EEPROM, SRAM is a volatile memory that will be erased if the power is turned off. The ATmega328P chip in the Arduino has the following memory capacities. In a flash 32 kilobits, SRAM is a company that makes semiconductors. 2,000 bytes 1k byte EEPROM

Examples

- Bridge: Use a web browser to access the board's pins.
- ASCII Table for the Console: This shows how to print different formats to a Console.
- Console Pixel: Use the Console to control an LED.

- Console Read: Parse and repeat information from the Console.
- Datalogger: Save sensor data to an SD card.
- File Create Script: This shows how to use the process to write and run a shell script.
- HTTP Client: Make a basic client that downloads and outputs a site to the serial monitor.
- HTTP Client Console: Using Console, create a basic client which downloads a site and outputs it to a serial monitor.
- Mailbox Read Messages: Use a browser to send messages to an Arduino microcontroller using the REST API.
- Process: Shows how to perform Linux commands using process.

5.2 EEPROM Library

Enables reading and writing to the permanent board storage

- EEPROM Clear: The bytes inside the EEPROM are cleared.
- EEPROM Read: It Reads the details of the EEPROM and transfers them to the PC.
- EEPROM Write: Writes values to the EEPROM from an analog input.
- EEPROM Crc: Computes the CRC of the contents of an EEPROM chip as if it were an array.
- EEPROM Get: Gets values from an EEPROM and displays them on serial as floats.
- EEPROM Iteration: Learn how to iterate over the memory regions of an EEPROM.
- EEPROM Put: Using variable semantics, write values to EEPROM.

- EEPROM Update: Increases EEPROM life by storing values read from A0 in EEPROM and only writing the value if it differs.

5.3 Esplora Library

Allows simple access to the Esplora's many sensors and actuators.

- Esplora Accelerometer: It Read the accelerometer's readings.
- Esplora Blink: A Esplora's RGB LED will blink.
- Esplora Joystick Mouse: Control the mouse on your computer using Esplora's Joystick.
- Esplora LED Show: Make a light show with LED using the Joystick and slider.
- Esplora Led Show 2: Change the color of the onboard LED using the mic, light sensor and linear potentiometer on the Esplora.
- Esplora Light Calibrator: Check and calibrate the light sensor on the Esplora.
- Esplora Music: Use the Esplora to make some music.
- Esplora Kart: Play the kart racing game using the Esplora as just a controller.
- Esplora Pong: Use Processing to play Pong with Esplora.
- Esplora Remote: Control the outputs by connecting the Esplora to Processing.
- Esplora Tabular: Print the information from its Esplora sensor in a table style.

5.4 Ethernet Library

It is possible to connect to a network (both local and Internet) to use the Arduino Ethernet circuit or shield.

- Advanced Chat Server: Create a straightforward chat server.

- Barometric Pressure HTTP Server: Provides a web page with the readings from the barometric pressure sensor.
- Chat Server: Create a basic chat server.
- DHCP Address Printer: Use DHCP to get an IP address and print it out.
- Dhcp Chat Server: This is a very basic DHCP Chat Server.
- Telnet Client: This is a very basic Telnet client.
- UDP Send/Receive String: Use UDP to receive and send text strings.

5.5 SD Library

Allows you to read and write to SD cards.

- Card Info: Displays information about the SD card.
- Datalogger: Use an SD card to store data from three analog sensors.
- Dump File it Read a document from the Memory card.
- Files: Create and delete a file on an SD card.
- List Files: Print a directory on an SD card's files.
- Read Write: Access data stored on an SD card by reading and writing to it.

5.6 Servo Library

Arduino boards may be used to operate several different servo motors.

- Potentiometer: A potentiometer is used to track the direction of a servo.
- Sweep: A servo motor's shaft is swept back and forth.

5.7 SPI Library

Allows communication using devices that utilize the SPI (Serial Peripheral Interface) bus.

- Barometric Pressure Sensor: Use the SPI protocol to read air temperature and pressure from a sensor.

- Digital Potentiometer Control: Use the SPI protocol to control an AD5206 digital potentiometer.

5.8 Stepper Library

Arduino boards can operate a wide range of stepper motors.

- Motor Knob: A potentiometer is used to control a very precise stepper motor.

- Stepper One Revolution: Rotate the shaft clockwise and counterclockwise one revolution.

- Stepper One Step at a Time: Rotate the shaft one step to ensure the motor is properly wired.

- Stepper Speed Control: A potentiometer is used to control the stepping speed.

Conclusion

This short book, my friends, has already come to an end. Although I hope that Arduino programming will be "off the shelf" in your sector, you will be happy if it only piques your curiosity. This book's ideas are among the most effective approaches for Arduino programmers of all levels to increase their performance and skill. Think about how you and your colleagues will use them and other technologies that will become accessible to increase productivity. This book is for Arduino beginners and experts who wish to learn how to program the board from scratch. The following subject, which is equally significant for beginners and pros, has been tried to be covered in this book.

- Make sure you have the right Arduino hardware and peripherals for your project.
- Connect your Arduino to the Arduino IDE after downloading and installing it.
- Quickly and simply create, develop, upload, and run your first Arduino program.
- Know C grammar, decision-making, strings, data structures, and functions.
- Use pointers to work with memory and avoid common mistakes.
- Add development and testing environments to your Arduino and development and testing shields and functionality electronics.
- Send output and publish input from analog devices or digital interfaces using existing hardware library functions or creating your own
- Put together an Ethernet shield, an Ethernet cable, and a networking application.

Arduino Programming

A Complete Guide to Master Tools and Techniques On
Getting Started With Arduino

By

Robert Campbell

Introduction

An Arduino is a microcontroller development board that is open-source. In layman's terms, the Arduino may be used to control and read sensors, motors and lights. It enables you to upload programs to the board, which can subsequently interact with real-world objects. You may use this to create gadgets that respond to and respond to the outside environment. For example, if a humidity sensor linked to a plant pot becomes too dry, you may activate an automated watering system. You may also create a standalone chat server that is connected to your internet network. You can also set it to tweet whenever your cat enters or exits a pet door. You may also set your alarm to prepare a cup of coffee whenever you wake up. If anything is controlled by electricity in any way, the Arduino can interact with it somehow. Even if it isn't run on electricity, you can usually utilize items that are (such as motors and electromagnets) to interact with it. The Arduino's capabilities are almost unlimited.

Important essential features and applications of Arduino will be covered in this book.

- Description of the Arduino Board

- Installation of an Arduino

- Structure of the Arduino Program

- Data Types for Arduino

- Arduino Constants & Variables

- Arduino Programmers

- Arduino Statements of Control

- Loops for Arduino

- Arduino's Features

- Strings for Arduino

- String Object for Arduino

- Arrays on Arduino

- And there are many more.

Chapter-1 Overview of Arduino?

Arduino is a free source programming circuit board used in several basic and complicated maker space projects. This board has a microcontroller that may be designed to detect and control items in the real world. The Arduino may interact with various outputs, including LEDs and displays, by responding to sensors and inputs. Due to its flexibility and low cost, Arduino has become a popular choice for makers and maker spaces looking to create interactive hardware projects. Massimo Bansi launched Arduino in 2005 in Italy as a method for non-engineers to use a low-cost, easy-to-use tool for making hardware projects. Because the panel is accessible for free, it is distributed by an Open-Source license, allowing anybody to make their own. Many Arduino board clones and modifications accessible on the internet; however, only authorized boards contain Arduino in their name. You'll go through a couple of Arduino boards present and how they vary in the following section.

1.1 Integrated Development Environment

Arduino is an open-source prototyping platform with simple hardware and software. It comprises a programable circuit board (also known as a microcontroller) and ready-to-use software known as the Arduino IDE (Integrated Development Environment), which is used to create and upload computer code to the physical board.

- Arduino boards can take analog or digital data input from various sensors and convert them to an output, such as starting a motor, turning on/off LEDs, connecting to the cloud, and various other functions.

- You may use the Arduino IDE to control the functionalities of your board by sending a list of instructions to a board's microcontroller (uploading software is referred).

- Unlike most prior customizable integrated circuits, Arduino does not require the use of a separate piece of hardware (known as a programmer) to load fresh code into the board.

- Moreover, the Arduino IDE employs a simpler model of C++, making it simpler to learn how to program. • Finally, Arduino offers a standard modular design that divides the microcontroller's functionality into a much more accessible packaging.

1.2 Applications of Arduino

For embedded system applications, Arduino is a breeze to utilize. Because of the Arduino open-source software, folks who do not have excellent programming abilities but want to collaborate on embedded system projects may simply utilize Arduino to build their embedded system-based projects. To start with Arduino, you need a basic understanding of electronics, such as utilizing resistors, capacitors, transistors, diodes, and other fundamental electrical components. But don't worry if you don't know anything about electronics. In the upcoming chapter of this book, you will discover all there is to know about Arduino. The following are a few Arduino applications:

- Robotics
- GSM based projects
- Ethernet-based projects
- WIFI
- Bluetooth
- And a variety of additional topics.

1.3 Types of Arduino Boards

Arduino is a fantastic platform for developing ideas and innovations, but choosing the proper board may be difficult. If you're new to Arduino, you may have assumed that there's just one "Arduino" board, and that was it. In truth, there are several versions of the genuine Arduino boards and hundreds of clones from rivals. But don't worry; later in this chapter, you will learn which one to start with. The following are some examples of the many kinds of Arduino boards available. The authentic Arduino boards are those with the Arduino logo on them, although there are many excellent clones on the marketplace. One of the main reasons to purchase a clone is that they are usually less costly than the original. For example, Spark Fun and Adafruit provide Arduino boards less expensive but have the same quality as the originals. One word of caution, be cautious when purchasing boards from unknown vendors.

Another thing to think about when picking a board is indeed the sort of project you want to accomplish. If you want to make a wearable electrical project, the Lilypad boards from Spark fun are a good option. The Lilypad is intended to be sewed into wearable and e-textiles crafts with ease. If your work has a compact form factor, the Arduino Pro Mini, which has a very tiny footprint comparing to other boards, can be a good choice. For analysis and analysis of the top boards available, see Spark fun's Arduino Comparison Guide. Following that, we'll look at our preferred Arduino board, which is suggested novices begin with.

Arduino Uno

The Arduino Uno is among the most famous Arduino boards. Even though it was not the first board to be launched, it is still the most popular and well-documented on the market. Because of its widespread usage, the Arduino Uno has many projects and forums available on the internet to assist you in getting started or getting out of a bind. Because of its amazing features and simplicity of use, You love the Uno.

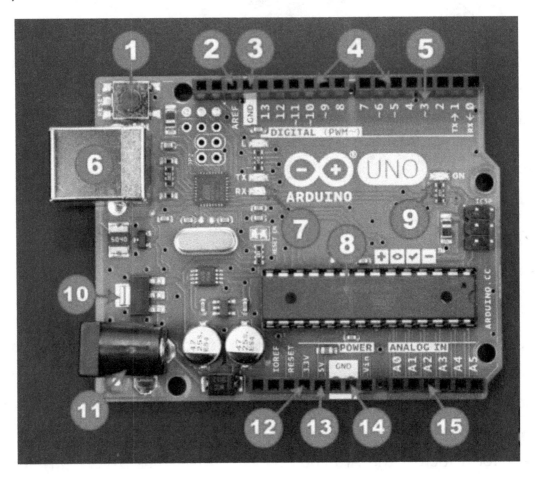

Breakdown of the Board

The components that comprise an Arduino UNO board are listed below, along with their functionalities.

- **Reset Button.** Pressing this button will reload any programming on the Arduino board.

- **AREF.** This acronym stands for "Analog Reference," which establishes an outside reference voltage.

- **Ground Pin**. The Arduino has many ground pins, all of which function in the same way.

- **PWM.** The pins indicated with the () symbol may emulate analog output.

- **USB Cable.** Used to power up the Arduino and upload programs.

- **TX/RX.** LEDs that indicate data transmission and reception.

- **AT Mega Microchip.** It is the brain of the board, which is where the programs are kept.

- **Power Indicator Light**. When the board is hooked into a power source, this LED illuminates.

- **Voltage Regulator.** It regulates the voltage supplied to an Arduino board.

- **3.3 volts Pin.** The Pin offers 3.3 hours of electricity to your work.

- **Dc Voltage Barrel Jack.** This Pin is used to power the Arduino with such a power source.

- **V Pin**. This Pin provides your projects with 5 volts of electricity.

- **Ground Pins.** The Arduino has several ground pins that all function the same way.

- **Analog Pins**. The pins can read analog sensor signals and transform them too digital.

Arduino Power Supply

The Arduino Uno requires a power supply to function and may be charged in several ways. You may connect the boards directly to your desktop using a USB connection, as most users do. Consider utilizing a 9V rechargeable battery to power your project if you want it to be portable. The last option is to utilize a 9V AC source of power.

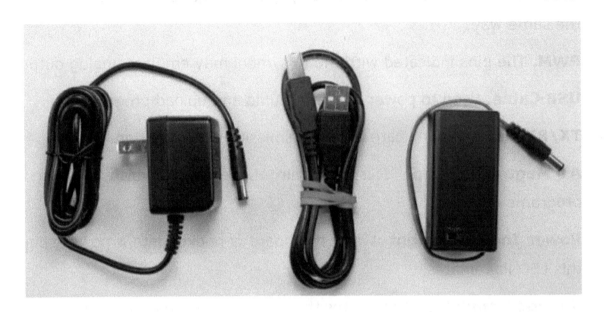

Arduino Breadboard

When working with Arduino, a solderless breadboard is also essential. You may use this gadget to develop your Arduino work without having to connect the circuit permanently. You may make additional prototypes and test with alternative circuit designs using a breadboard. Metal clips are joined via a strip of conductive material within the plastic housing slots (tie points).

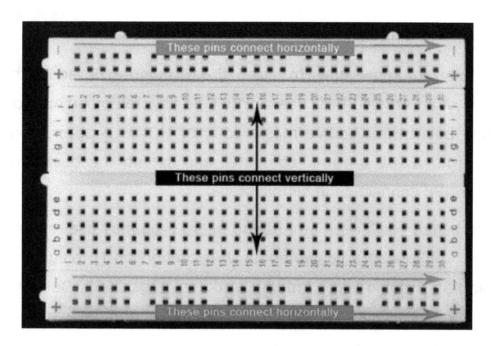

On a separate note, the breadboard does not have its power supply and must be connected to the Arduino board via jumper wires. These fibers are also used to link resistors, switches, and other elements to make the circuit.

1.4 How to Program Arduino

You'll have to upload the software (also called a sketch) to an Arduino after the circuit has also been built on the breadboard. The sketch is a collection of instructions that instructs the board on what tasks it must do. At any one moment, an Arduino board could only hold and execute one program. The IDE, which means for Integrated Development Environment, is the software used to build Arduino sketches. There are two essential aspects to any Arduino sketch:

void setup (). Sets up items that only need to be performed once and then aren't repeated.

Void loop (). This section contains instructions that will be repeated until the circuit is shut off.

1.5 Arduino – Installation

You are ready to know how to start the Arduino IDE and other major components of an Arduino UNO board. You'll be able to upload our software to the Arduino board after You've mastered this. In this chapter, you'll try to install an Arduino IDE on your computer and set up the board to get the program via USB connection in simple steps.

1st step, to begin, you'll need an Arduino board (you may use any board) and a USB wire. You'll need a conventional USB connection (A plug to B plug) if you're using an Arduino UNO, Arduino, Arduino Mega 2560, Duemilanove, or Diecimila. If you're using an Arduino Nano, you'll need to have an A to B cable instead, as seen in the picture below.

Download Arduino IDE Software.

From the Arduino Official Website's Download page, you may download several versions of the Arduino IDE. You must choose software that is appropriate for the OS (IOS, Windows or Linux). Unzip the file after it has finished downloading.

Power up your board.

The Duemilanove, Arduino Uno, Mega, and Nano automatically take power from the computer's USB port or an additional power source. If you're using the Arduino Diecimila, make sure it's set up to take power from the USB port. A jumper, a little bit of plastic that slips into two out of the three ports between the power and USB connections, is used to choose the power source. Make sure it's connected to the two pins nearest to the USB cable. Using the USB cable, attach the board to the computer. The PWR (power) LED (green) should light up.

Launch Arduino IDE.

You must unzip the folder after downloading the Arduino IDE program. The program icon with an infinite label may be found within the folder (application.exe). To launch the IDE, double-click the icon.

Open your first project.

You have two choices after the software has started:

- Begin working on a new project.

- Select a pre-existing project as an example.

- Select file>> New to start a new project.

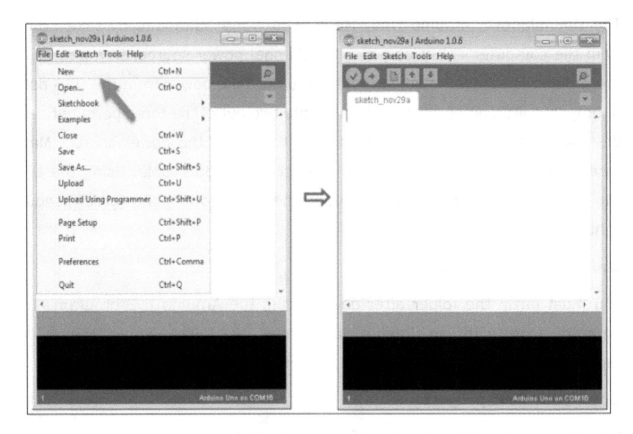

Select File >> Example >> Basics >> Blink to open an existing work example. You've chosen only one of the Blink instances for this example. It uses a timer to switch the LED off and on. Some other examples from the list may be chosen.

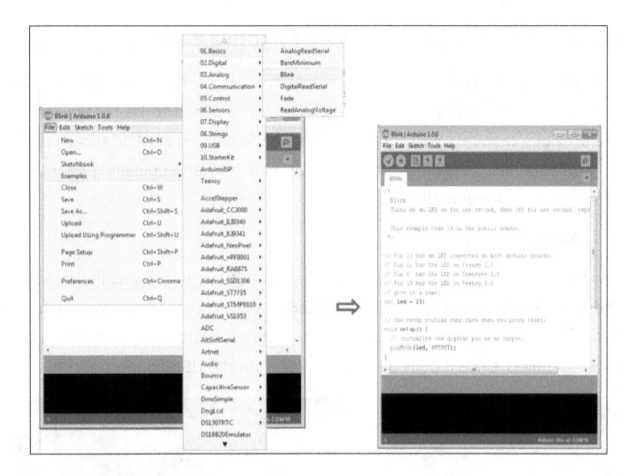

Select your Arduino board.

You must pick the right Arduino board name that matches the board linked to your computer to prevent errors when uploading your software to the board. Select your board from Tools >> Board.

Chapter-2 Basic Concepts of programming

You have learned how to install your Arduino IDE, configure the appropriate USB drivers, and set up the IDE for all the Arduino Uno to be recognized in the previous chapter. We'll continue working with Arduino IDE in this chapter by examining its capabilities, learning how to use it, and uploading your first program to an Arduino UNO board.

2.1 Arduino IDE

Connect the Arduino Board to a computer via USB connection as indicated in the picture below and pick the proper board & COM port if not previously done before continuing with the chapter. The Arduino board does not need any external power since it pulls all of its power from the USB connection.

Sketches are the programs that run in the Arduino environment. The white region indicated in the figure below is the Text Editor in the Arduino IDE. It is where You'll write all of the code on our Arduino boards. Before you get too excited and start developing your program, you'll have a look at an example sketch included in Arduino IDE. To do so, go to the "File" menu and choose the "Examples" option. You can see a list of appropriately classified examples in the dropdown of the Examples tab, such as Basic, Analog, Digital, Communication, and so on.

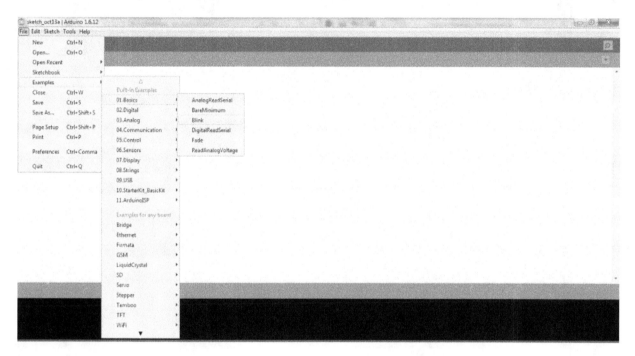

Use the simple example as a beginning or first-time user, and then pick the "Blink" sketch. The Blink drawing will be shown in a new window. You will use the Blink sketch to turn on the LED attached to the Arduino's 13th Pin for one second and then switch it off for a second in a repeating manner, i.e., you will blink the LED continually.

When You first start learning about electronics and microcontrollers, the first project or program you do is flash an LED, since flashing an LED in electronics is akin to typing Hello World in C. You will post the drawing without delving more into the programming portion of the project at this time. you need to utilize two icons in the Arduino IDE to upload the program to the Arduino board: the first is "Verify or Compile," and the second is "Upload." In the figure below, certain symbols are highlighted.

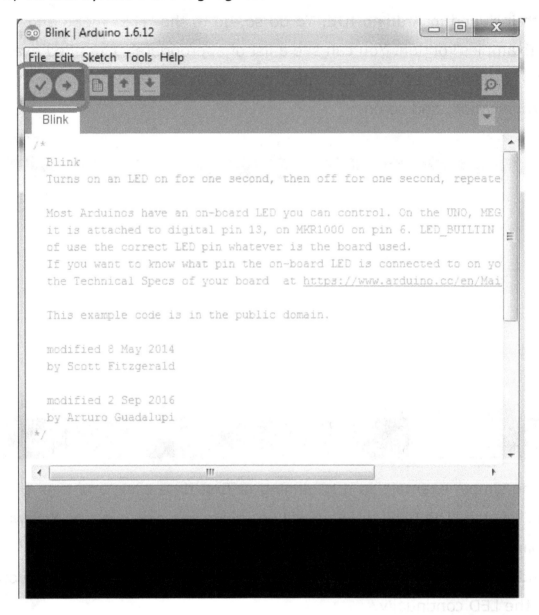

The Check or Compile symbol is the first symbol with a checkmark. You may use this icon to see whether the provided sketch is valid in terms of syntax and to see if there would be any compilation issues. You only post the drawing if the compiling is complete and error-free. To check or build the drawing, you may utilize the keyboard Ctrl + R.

The Message window is placed at the base of the IDE. It shows the compilation status, error warnings, and the specifics of the faults. You can see the progress of the compilation and the Done compiling message, and in the message window, you compile the sketch using the first icon.

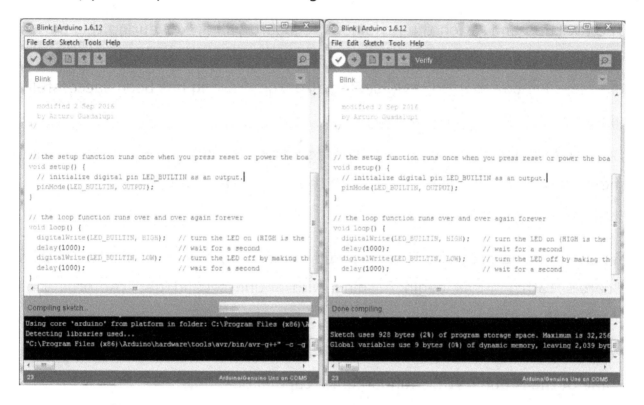

The compilation pauses at that moment if there is an issue in the sketch, such as a missing an unclosed bracket or semicolon, and the message pane displays the error with its kind and position. You may rectify the mistake using this method.

The Upload symbol is the second symbol next to the Verify symbol. Once the drawing has been successfully compiled, you may use this icon to submit it. The compiled drawing may be uploaded using the shortcut Ctrl + U. The drawing is constructed before uploading whenever You click the Upload button.

You may proceed with submitting our drawing now that it has been successfully compiled with no issues. When You click the upload tab, the sketch begins to upload, and the Arduino board's microcontroller is programmed.

The RX LEDs and TX on the Arduino UNO board will flicker during this period to indicate that data is being transferred over the serial connection. Notice in the message box that Done Uploading after the drawing has been successfully uploaded.

Other information shown in the message box includes the quantity of flash memory used by the code, the time it took to upload, and so on.

As soon as the program is successfully uploaded, the LED on the Arduino Board's 13th Pin will begin flashing with a one-second gap (According to the sketch written).

You learned how to upload your first sketch to the Arduino Board and about some of the Arduino IDE's fundamental capabilities.

2.2 Arduino Program Analysis

You saw how to configure the Arduino IDE, build (or validate) the code, upload the program to an Arduino UNO board, and verify for error messages in the earlier section of the book. All of this was shown with the aid of the Arduino IDE's sample program "Blink."

You'll attempt to comprehend the Blink program, its components, its syntax, and some preset functions in this chapter. You will also experiment with modifying the basic Blink sketch to see how they affect the output.

To do so, launch the blink program in the Arduino IDE (and with Arduino Board currently attached to the computer). You can notice some grey lines at the top of the drawing and some colorful lines at the draw base. Each Arduino sketch (or, for that matter, any program, regardless of programming language) is made up of a series of reference lines called comments and the actual code.

2.3 Arduino Code for Beginners

C++ is the Arduino programming language. The majority of the time, users will utilize a limited subset of C++ that resembles C. If you're acquainted with Java, you'll find C++ to be simple to use and understand. Do not be concerned or worried if you've never coded before. You'll find everything you have to get started in the next paragraphs. C++'s most significant "high-level" feature is that this is object-oriented. An object is a concept in such a language that mixes functional code (code that performs computations and memory operations) with "state" code (the results of such simple values or calculations stored in variables).

Compared to previous paradigms, object orientation enabled programming to be somewhat more productive in certain applications since it enabled programmers to design complex programs using abstractions.

An Ethernet adapter, for example, might be represented as an object with properties (such as its IP and MAC addresses) and capabilities (like asking a DHCP server for network configuration details). Object-oriented programming became the most popular programming paradigm, and C++ has had a significant effect on most current languages, including Java, Ruby, and Python. You'll be referring to libraries containing object definitions (called "classes") in a lot of the sketch code you'll be authoring and viewing. Your original code will be made up of "glue" code and modifications to a significant degree. By studying a tiny part of C++, you can indeed be productive nearly immediately.

The code that comprises your sketch must be turned into machine code which the Arduino's microcontroller understands. A compiler is a particular software that does the compilation. You don't have to worry more about intricacies since the Arduino IDE comes with just an open-source C++ compiler. Consider this: once you click the "Upload" button, the IDE launches the compiler, which turns your human-readable instructions into ones and zeros before sending it all to the microcontroller through USB.

C++, like any other effective programming language, has a variety of terms and constructions. Constructors, operators, Conditionals, functions, data structures, variables, and many other things are available.

You will learn about the architecture of an Arduino program, functions, and variables in this chapter. Take a few moments to absorb this new information before moving on to the last session, in that you will understand how to program the Arduino to make choices and communicate with the outside environment.

2.4 An Arduino sketch

The simplest Arduino sketch imaginable is

```
void setup(){

printf("hello"); // setup code, run once:

}

void loop(){

printf("hello"); // main code run repeatedly:

}
```

There are two functions in this code.

- The first one has been put up (). When the program begins, everything you enter in this function would be performed either by Arduino just once.

- Loop is the second (). When the Arduino finishes executing the instructions in the setup () method, it will enter a loop () and continue executing it in a loop until you reboot it or turn off the power.

Take note of the close and open parenthesis in setup () and loop (). Functions may accept arguments, which allows the program to communicate information across its many functions. There are no arguments supplied to the loop and setup procedures. If you put anything inside the parenthesis, the compiler will report a compile error and halt the compilation process. Even if you don't utilize them, these two functions will be present in every drawing you produce.

Removing one of them will result in an error notice from the compiler. These are two of the Arduino language's minimal requirements. The two functions are essential, but you may create your own if you like. Let's have a look at the following point.

2.5 Custom functions

A function is nothing more than a collection of instructions with such a name. The Arduino IDE requires your sketch to have the loop () and setup () routines, but you may create your own. Organizing your drawings by grouping instructions within functions is an excellent idea, particularly as they grow more complex as you gain confidence as a programmer. A definition and the code that fits within the curly brackets are required to define a function. At least the following is included in the definition.

- one return type

- a name

- a parameter list

```
int calc(int x, int y)
{
    int z = x + y;
    return z;
}
```

In the first line, the return type is int. It instructs the compiler that the caller will get an integer value (the function Called).

The function's name (also referred to as its "identifier") is doing a calc. You may name the functions anything you want as long as you don't use a reserved term (that is, a term already in use by the Arduino language), there are no spaces, and special characters like percent, $, and # aren't used. A number cannot be used as the initial character. If in doubt, keep in mind that function names should only include numbers, letters, and the underscore.

You establish a new integer-type variable during the first line of the coding (int). The result of adding x and y is assigned to z.

Finally, you return the value saved in z to the caller of calc in the two lines of the function's body. Let's imagine you want to use your setup function to call calc. Here's a detailed example of how to accomplish it:

```
void setup()
{
    // setup code, to run only once:
    int z = calc(8,12);
```

```
}

void loop()

{

  // main code, to execute it repeatedly:

}

int calc(int x, int y)

{

  int z = x + y;

  return z;

}
```

The second line of the setup () method declares a variable, x. It calls the method calc on the same line and sends the numbers 8 and 12 to it. The calc function adds the two integers together and delivers the result 3 to a caller, the setup () method's second line. The number 20 is then saved in variable z, and the setup () method is completed.

2.6 Comments

Comments can be found on any line that begins with / or paragraph (contain multiply lines) that begin with /* and end with */. The compiler disregards comments. They are intended for the coder to read. Comments are being used to explain how code works or leave remarks for other developers (or self).

There is indeed a definition of a parameter with the identifier in the setup () method. There is also a definition of a variable with the same identifier in function calc (The fact that this definition is on the function definition block makes no difference).). It's not an issue to have variables to the same name as long as they're not even in the same target. The curly brackets determine the scope. Within that scope would be any variable between being an open and closed curly bracket. There is no contradiction if there is indeed a variable with the same name declared in another scope.

When choosing a name for the variables, be cautious. Scope issues may be a pain: you can think a variable is available at a certain point in your sketch just to discover it is out of range. Also, make sure your variables have appropriate descriptive names. If you wish to save the value of a pin in a variable, name it something like:

```
int p = 0; // p should be replacing with pin,
```

2.7 Data Types

In C, data types refer to a comprehensive system for defining variables and functions of various kinds. The category of a variable dictates how much storage space it takes up and how the stored bit pattern is interpreted. The table below lists all of the data categories that you'll encounter when programming with Arduino.

void

Only function declarations utilize the void keyword. It denotes that the function should return no data to the function of which it was invoked.

Example

```
Void Loop (){
    // Set of code should be written here.
}
```

Boolean

True (1) or false (0) are the only two possible values for a Boolean. One byte of storage memory is used for each Boolean variable.

Example

`boolean val = false;` // declaration, initial value of variable be false

`boolean state = true;` // declaration, initial value of state be True

Char

A character value is stored in the data type, which takes up a single byte of memory. Single quotes are used for character literals, such as 'A,' while double quotes are used for strings with several characters, such as "ABC."

Characters, on the other hand, are kept as integers. In the ASCII chart, you can observe the particular encoding. It implies that mathematical operations on characters may be performed using the ASC-II value of the character. Because the ASC-II forms of capital character A are 65, 'A' + 1 also has 66.

Example

`Char xhar1 = 'a'` ;// declaration, initial value of variable(char) be a

`Char xhar1= 97` ;// declaration, initial value of variable(char) be 97

unsigned char

It is also an unsigned type of data with a one-byte memory footprint. Numbers ranging from 0 to 255 are encoded using unsigned char data type.

Example

Unsigned Char Xchar1 = 225; // declaration, initial value of variable(char) be a 225

byte

A byte stores an 8-bit unsigned number, from 0 to 255.

Example

`byte m = 25;`//declaration of a variable with type byte and initialize it.

int

Integers are the most used data type for storing numbers. A 16-bits (2-byte) result is calculated in int. It results in -32,768 - 32,767 (with a minimum of -2^{15} and a maximum of (2^{15}) - 1).

The int size changes depending on the board. An int, for example, on the Arduino Due saves a 4-byte (32-bit) value. The result ranges from -2147483648 - 2,147,483,647 (with a minimum of -2^{31} and a maximum of (2^{31}) - 1).

`int num1 = 232 ;`// declaration, initial value of variable(int) be 232

Unsigned int

Unsigned ints hold a two-byte value in the same manner as ints do. They don't store negative integers, instead just positive ones, giving them a usable range of 0- 65,535 (2^{16}) - 1. The Due saves a four-byte (32-bit) value that may range from 0-4,294,967,295 (2^{32} - 1) value.

`Unsigned int numbr1 = 560;` // declaration, initial value of variable(int) be 560

Word

A word holds a 16-bits unsigned number on the Arduino and other ATMEGA-based devices. It saves a 32-bits unsigned integer on the Due or Zero.

Example

`word x = 5160 ;`// declaration, initial value of variable(word) be 5160

Long

Long variables hold 32 bits (4 bytes) and range-2,147,483,648-2,147,483,647, are enhanced size variables for number storage.

Example

`Long speed = 589696`; / declaration, initial value of variable(long) be 589696

short

A 16-bit data type is referred to as a short. A brief saves a 16-bit (2-byte) value on all Arduinos (ARM and AT-Mega based). It results in a range of -32,768 - 32,767 (with a minimum of -2^{15} and a maximum of $(2^{15}) - 1$).

Example

`short num = 114;` / declaration, initial value of variable(long) be 114

float

A number with a decimal point is the data type for a floating-point number. Because it offers more resolution than integers, floating-point integers are often employed to approximate analog and continuous quantities.

Floating-point numbers may range in size from 3.4028235E+38 - -3.4028235E+38. They are represented as 32 bits of data (4 bytes).

Example

`float pi = 3.14;` /declaration of a float variable with 3.14 as its initial value

double

Double-precision floating-point numbers take up four bytes on the Uno and other ATMEGA-based boards. That is, a double implementation is identical to the float implementation, with no increased inaccuracy. Doubles mostly on Arduino Due have an 8-bytes which is equal to (64-bit) precision.

Example.

```
double num = 256.342;/ declare a double variable and initialize it with
256.342
```

2.8 Variables

When it comes to data processing, a program is really handy. Data processing is something that programs perform all of the time. Either a user will provide data for the program to process or generate its data (possibly via a keypad). From a sensor (such as a temperature thermistor), the network (such as a cloud computer), a local shared folder (such as a Memory Card), a local memory (such as an EPROM), and a variety of additional locations.

Regardless of where your software obtains its data, it must keep it in memory to function with it. Variables are used to do this. A variable is indeed equipment that assigns a name to a memory region (an identifier). You utilize an easy-to-remember moniker instead of the memory location's address in our software. You've previously encountered a variable. You have created several variables, x, y, and z, containing an integer in the previous section on custom functions.

Other than numbers, variables may contain a variety of data. A couple of these are built-in to the Arduino language (that, recall, is C++).

A valid name and type are required to create a variable. A valid name has an underscore, letters, and numbers that begin with a character and is not reserved, much like functions. Here's an illustration:

```
byte sensor_B_value;
```

This line creates the sensor_B_value variable, which will store a single byte into memory. You may store data in it in the following way:

```
sensor_B_value = 1596;
```

This value may be printed to a serial monitor as follows:

```
serial.print(sensor_B_value);
```

The serial display is an Arduino IDE feature that enables you to show text from the Arduino on your screen. You will go into more detail about this later, but for now, you want to demonstrate how to access the hash value in a variable. Simply say its name. Remember what you said about scope earlier: the variable must be inside scope once it is invoked.

A variable's value may also be changed, which is one of its most appealing features. You may update the variable by taking a fresh reading from the sensor as follows:

```
sensor_B_value = 221;
```

There's no issue; the old value has vanished, and the new value has been saved.

2.9 Constants

If there is a value in your drawing that will not change, label it as a constant. Constants provide memory and processing performance advantages, and it is a good practice to employ them. You may use the following syntax to declare a constant:

```
const int sen_pin = 0;
```

You give the variable sen_pin a name, indicate that as constant, and setting it to 0. You'll receive a compiler error warning if you attempt to alter the value later.

Operators

O Operators are functions that act on a single or several bits of data.

The fundamental arithmetic operations, = (assign), +, -, *, and /, are recognisable to most individuals. There are, however, many more. The following are some of the most regularly used operators: The software will not be uploaded to an Arduino at all.

"%" Modulo

It is a mathematical operator in which remainder is returned after division

Consider the following scenario: 5% 2 = 1

+=, -=, *=, /= Compound operator.

It executes the code on a variable's current value.

Example

```
int x = 15;  x+= 3;
```

Consequently, a containing 18 will be produced (the original 15 plus a three from the addition operation).

++, --

It will increase or decrease the value of a variable by 1

Example

```
int x = 15; x++;
```

The answer will be 16.

Comparison operators. ==, !=, <, >, <=, >=

Based on the comparison result, comparison operators will produce a Boolean (true or false).

== means equality

! = means un-equality

< means less than

> means greater than

<= means less than or equal to

>= means greater than or equal t.

Example

```
int x = 15;
```

```
int y== 6;
```

Boolean x = y == z; As a consequence, variable c will have a false (0) boolean value. The compound assignment operators will always give true (1) and false (0) results.

NOT (!), AND (&&), OR (||)

Operators that are logical. Using the "!" operator, you may reverse a boolean value. && AND of two Booleans || OR of two Booleans ||. AND give 1 means true all all the inputs variable are 1 or true otherwise false. OR operation will give 0 or false if all the input variables is zero or false.

```
boolean x = true;
```

```
boolean y = true;
```

```
boolean z = false;
```

```
boolean a = !x; // a  will give false
```

```
boolean b = y && x; // b will give false
```

```
boolean c = y || z; // z  will give true
```

There are others as well. Bitwise operators may be used to operate at the bit level, such as manipulating individual bits inside a byte (which is helpful for stuff like shift registers). However, that's something you may learn afterward.

Chapter-3: I/O Functions

The Arduino board's pins can be used as both inputs or outputs. We'll go through how the pins operate in various modes. It's worth noting that most Arduino analog pins can be set and utilized in the same way as digital pins can.

3.1 Pins as INPUT

When utilizing Arduino pins as inputs, they are already set up as inputs and do not have to be explicitly designated as inputs using pinMode(). High-impedance pins are those that have been configured in this manner. Input pins place incredibly low requirements on the circuit they're sampling, the equivalent of a 100 megaohm series resistor at the front of the Pin.

It implies that switching the input pin from one state to the other requires relatively little current. As a result, the pins may build a touch sensor or scan a LED as just a photodiode.

With nothing attached to it or wires attached to It that are not linked to other circuits, pins set as pinMode (Pin, INPUT) report random adjustments in pin state, taking up electrical distortion from the environment capacitively connecting the state of a neighboring pin.

3.2 Pull-up Resistors

When no input is provided, the pull-up resistor is often used to guide input signals to the predefined condition. On the input, a pull-up resistance (to +5V) or a pull-down resistor (to ground) may be used to accomplish this. For just a pull-down or pull-up resistor, a 10K ohm resistor is an excellent choice.

3.3 Pull-up Resistor as Input

The At-mega chip has 20,000 pull-up resistors that may be accessed by software. Set the pinMode() to INPUT PULL-UP to access the built-in pull-up resistors. It reverses the behavior of an INPUT mode, in which HIGH indicates that the sensor is turned off and LOW indicates that it is turned on. The pull-value up's is determined by the microcontroller utilized. The value of most AVR-based boards is certified to be between $20,000 and $50,000. It is between 50k and 150k on the Arduino Due. Consult the datasheet for the microcontroller of your board for the specific value.

When attaching a sensor to an INPUT PULL-UP pin, make sure the other end is connected to the ground. It enables the Pinto to indicate HIGH whenever the switch is turned off and LOW because it is pushed in a basic switch. The pull-up resistors supply enough current to illuminate an LED attached to an input pin faintly. It is most likely what is going on if LEDs inside a design seem to be operating, but only very weakly.

The pull-up resistors are controlled by the same registers (internal chip location) that control whether a bit is HIGH or LOW. As a result, if a pin is also programmed to have pull-up resistors when in input mode, the Pin will be set as HIGH when moved to an OUTPUT mode using pinMode (). If an output pin is set in a HIGH state and switched to an input using pinMode, the pull-up resistor will be set ().

```
pinMode(5,INPUT) ;
```
// <set pin as input not with the help of built resistor>

```
pinMode(3,INPUT_PULLUP) ;
```
// <set pin as input not with the help of built resistor>

3.4 Pins as OUTPUT

Low-impedance pins are those that have been set as OUTPUT using pinMode(). It implies they can deliver a significant quantity of electricity to other circuits. Atmega pins may deliver up to 40 milliamps of electricity to external devices/circuits as a source (positive current) or sink (negative current). It is sufficient current to illuminate an LED (remember the series resistor) brilliantly or power several sensors, but not enough to power relays, motors or solenoids.

Attempting to power high-current devices from output pins may harm or kill the Pin's output transistors, as well as the Atmega chip as a whole. It often leads to a "dead" bit in the microcontroller, although the other chips continue to work properly. As a result, unless maximum current taken from the pins is necessary for a specific application, it is a smart option to link the OUTPUT pins to many other devices with 470 or 1k resistors.

pinMode() Function

The pinMode() method is used to specify whether a pin should be utilized as an output or an input. The mode INPUT PULL-UP may be used to activate the internal pull-up resistors. In addition, the internal pull-ups are expressly disabled in the INPUT mode.

Syntax.   pinMode()

Example

```
Void setup(){pinMode(pin,mode);
}
```

- mode OUTPUT, INPUT, or INPUT_PULLUP
- pin the number of a pin which mode you want to change

```
int button=3 ; // button linked to pin 3
int LED=4; // LED linked to pin 4
void setup() {pinMode(button , INPUT_PULLUP);// input with pull-up resistor
pinMode(button,OUTPUT); // pin as output
}
void setup(){
If(digitalRead(button) == HIGH)
{
digitalWrite(LED,LOW);
delay(300); //300 ms delay
digitalWrite(LED,HIGH);
delay(300); //300 ms delay
}
}
```

digitalWrite() Function

To write a LOW or HIGH value to a digital pin, use the digitalWrite() method. If pinMode() has been used to establish the Pin as an OUTPUT, the voltage would be configured to the appropriate value, 5V (3.3V for 3.3V board) for HIGH, for LOW 0V (ground) If the Pin is set to INPUT, digitalWrite() will activate (HIGH) or deactivate (LOW) the input pin's internal pull-up. The internal pull-up resistance should be enabled by setting pinMode() to INPUT PULL-UP.

When executing digitalWrite(HIGH), if pinMode() is not set to OUTPUT, and an LED is connected to a pin, the LED may seem faint. DigitalWrite() will have activated the inbuilt pull-up resistor, which operates as a big current-limiting resistor if pinMode() is not explicitly set.

Syntax digitalWrite()

```
Void loop(){

digitalWrite(pin,value);

}
```

- PIN, which is the number of a pin which mode you want to change
- value, which is either HIGH or LOW

```
int LED = 3; // LED linked to pin 3

void setup( {

pin_Mode(LED,OUTPUT); // set as output

}

void setup(){

digitalWrite(LED,HIGH);

delay(300); // 300 ms delay

digitalWrite(LED,LOW);

delay(500); // 500 ms delay

}
```

analogRead( ) function

The digitalRead() method on the Arduino may detect if a potential is applied to its pins and display it. An off/no sensor (that senses the presence of an item) differs from an analog sensor, whose value changes constantly. A different sort of Pin is required to read this sort of sensor.

Six pins labeled "Analog In" are located in the lower-right corner of the Arduino board. These particular pins indicate whether or not potential is applied to it and the magnitude of that voltage. You may read the applied voltage to one of the pins using the analogRead() method. This method returns a value from 0 to 1023, corresponding to voltages of 0 to 5 volts. When a 2.5 V voltage is supplied to pin 0, for example, analogRead(0) returns 512.

Syntax analogRead()

```
analogRead(pin);
```

pin specifies the input pin pin to read via (0-7 on the Mini boards ,0-5 on most boards, 0-5 on the Mega)

Example

```
int analogPin=4;  //Linked to analog pin 3

int num = 0; // Store read value

void setup(){

  Serial.begin(8600); // setup

}

void loop() {

  num = analogRead(analogPin); // read the pin

  Serial.println(val); // debug

}
```

3.5 Arduino - Advanced I/O Function

Advanced output, as well as input functions will be covered.

Analogous Reference()

It is a function that returns a list of references

Configures the analog input reference voltage (the value used as the top of the input range). The possibilities are as follows:

- The default analogue reference is 5 volts (for 5V Arduino) or 3.3 v (on 3.3V Arduino) (on 3.3V Arduino)

- INTERNAL 1.1 volts upon on ATmega168 or ATmega328, and 3 volts on the ATmega8

- A built-in 1.1V reference, INTERNAL1V1 (Arduino Mega only)

- A built-in 3V reference is INTERNAL2V56 (Arduino Mega only)

- EXTERNAL The reference is the voltage provided to an AREF pin (0-5V only).

Syntax

- analogReference()

- analogReference (type);

Any kind of the following may be used (EXTERNAL, DEFAULT, INTERNAL2V56, INTERNAL, INTERNAL1V1)

The external voltage level mostly on the AREF pin should not be much less than 0V or greater than 5V. You should set the analog referencing to EXTERNAL before using the analogRead() method if you're utilizing an external level on the AREF pin. Otherwise, you risk harming your Arduino board's microprocessor by shorting the active voltage level (internally produced) and the AREF pin.

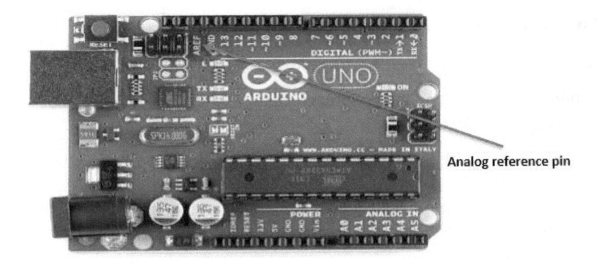

Analog reference pin

You may also use a 5K resistor to link the exterior voltage level to the AREF pin, enabling you to toggle among internally and externally reference voltages.

Because there are inbuilt 32K resistors on the AREF pin, the resistor will change the voltage used as the reference. The two works together to create a voltage divider. 2.5V passed via the resistor, for example, will result in 2.5*32/(32+5)=2.2V only at the AREF pin.

Example

```
int analogPin=4;
int num=0;
void setup(){
Serial.begin(9600);
analogReference(EXTERNAL
//reference.
}
```

```
void loop(){
val = analogRead(analogPin); // read the input pin
Serial.println(val); // debug value
}
```

3.6 Character Functions

All data is inputted into the computer as characters, including letters, numerals, or other special symbols. The abilities of C++ for analyzing and modifying individual characters are discussed in this chapter

Several methods in the character-handling library provide helpful checks or manipulations of specific types of data. As a parameter, each function gets a character, expressed as just an int, or EOF. Integers are often used to alter characters.

Remember that EOF is generally set to −1 and that certain hardware designs prohibit the storage of negative values in char variables. As a result, the character-handling routines work with characters as if they were integers.

The functionalities of the character-handling module are summarized in the table below. Include the cctype>>header while using operations from the character-handling library.

int isdigit(int x)

If x is a digit, it returns 1; otherwise, it returns 0.

int isalpha(int x)

If x is a letter, it returns 1; otherwise, it returns 0.

int isalnum(int x)

If x is a letter or digit, it returns 1; otherwise, it returns 0.

int isxdigit(int x)

If x is a hexadecimal digit, it returns 1; otherwise, it returns 0.

int islower(int x)

If x is a lowercase letter, it returns 1; otherwise, it returns 0.

int isupper(int x)

If x is an uppercase letter, it returns 1; otherwise, it returns 0.

int isspace(int x)

If x is a white-space character horizontal tab ('t'), (newline ('n'), form feed ('f'), carriage return ('r'), space (' '), vertical tab ('v'), it returns 1; otherwise, it returns 0.

int iscntrl(int x)

If x is a controlled character like horizontal tab ('t'), (newline ('n'), form feed ('f'), carriage return ('r'), space (' '), vertical tab ('v'), it returns 1; otherwise, it returns 0.

int ispunct(int x)

If x is a printed character apart from space, a numeral, or a letter, it returns 1; otherwise, it returns 0.

int isprint(int x)

If x is a printed character that includes a space (' '), it returns 1; otherwise, it returns 0.

int isgraph(int x)

If x is a printing letter apart from space (' '), it returns 1; otherwise, it returns 0.

Example

The functions isalnum, isdigit, isalpha, and isxdigit are shown in the following example. The isdigit function checks if the parameter is just a digit (0–9). The isalpha function detects if the parameter is an uppercase (A–Z) or lowercase (a–z) character. The isalnum function checks if the parameter is an uppercase, lowercase, or digit. If the input is a hexadecimal digit (A–F, a–f, 0–9), the function isxdigit returns true.

```
void setup(){

Serial.begin(9600);// Open the port at data rate to 9600 bps
Serial.print("\rIsdigit:\r");  // commants

Serial.print(isdigit('9')?"\r9":"9 not\r");

Serial.print("\rdigit\r"); //

Serial.print(isdigit('9')?"#is-a":"#is-not-a\r") ;

Serial.print("\rdigit\r");

Serial.print("\rIsalpha:\r" );

  Serial.print(isalpha('B' ) ?"A_is _a": "A_is _ot_a");

  Serial.print("letter\r");

  Serial.print(isalpha('B' ) ?"b_is_a": "b_is_not_a");

  Serial.print("letter\r");

  Serial.print(isalpha('B') ?"&_is_a": "&_is_not-a");

  Serial.print(" letter\r");
```

```
Serial.print(isalpha('B' )?"4_is_a":"4_is_not_a");

Serial.print("\rletter\r");

Serial.print("\risalnum:\r");

Serial.print(isalnum('A' ) ?"A_is_a":"A_is_not _a" );

Serial.print("digit_or_a_letter\r");

Serial.print(isalnum('8')?"\r8_is_a\r":"8_is_not_a");

Serial.print("\rdigit_or_a_letter\r");

Serial.print(isalnum('#')?" \r #is a":"#is_not_a\r ");

Serial.print("\r digit_or_ a_ letter\r");

Serial.print("\rIsxdigit:\r");

Serial.print(isxdigit('F')?" \r  F_is _a":"_ is _not a" );

Serial.print(" \r  hexadecimal_digit\r" );

Serial.print(isxdigit('J')?"J is a":"J_is_not-a");

Serial.print("\r  hexadecimal digit\r");

Serial.print(isxdigit('7')?"7_is_a":"7_is_not_a");

Serial.print(" \r  hexadecimal_digit\r");

Serial.print(isxdigit('$' )?" \r  $_is_a":"$_is_not_a" );

Serial.print(" \r  hexadecimal digit\r");

Serial.print(isxdigit('f )?" \r f_is_a":"f_is_not_a");

}

void loop () {

}
```

Result

Isdigit:

8 digit

not

Isalpha:

A_is_a_letter

B_is_a_letter

&_Is_not_a _etter

4_is_not_a_letter

isalnum:

A_is_a_digit_or_a_letter

8_is_a_digit_or_a_letter

#_is_not_a_digit_or_a_letter

isxdigit:

F_is_a_hexadecimal_digit

J_is_not_a_hexadecimal_digit

7_is_a_hexadecimal_digit

$_i_not_a_hexadecimal_digit

F_is_a_hexadecimal_digit

For each letter examined, You just use conditional operator (?:) to decide if the text " is a " or the phrase " is not a " should be written in the output. Line a, for example, shows that the text "8 is a " is written if '8' would be a digit—

that is when isdigit gives a true (non-zero) result. The text " 8 is not a " is written when '8' would not be a digit (i.e., when isdigit returns 0).

Chapter-4 Control Statements, Loops, Functions and Strings

You will learn control statements that control the flower of execution, a loop that executes a set of repeated statements in this chapter,.

4.1 Control Statements

The programmer must define one or more criteria to be examined or checked by the program using decision-making structures. It should be accompanied by the statements that will be performed if the condition is true, and optionally, additional statements will be performed if the condition is false.

The general shape of a common decision-making framework present in most programming languages is shown below.

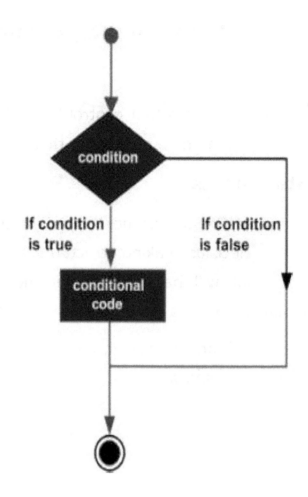

If statement

It accepts a parenthesis-enclosed phrase as well as a statement or set of statements. The block of statements or statements is performed if another expression is true; else, the statements are skipped.

If ...else statement

When the condition is false, an if statement might be preceded via an optional else statement.

If...else if ...else statement

When the condition is false, an if statement might be preceded via an optional else statement.

switch case statement

Switch...case, like if statements, regulates the flow of the program by letting programmers declare distinct instructions that should be performed under different circumstances.

Conditional Operator?

What's with the conditional operator? In C, there is just one ternary operator.

4.2 Loops

Different control structures are available in programming languages, allowing for more sophisticated execution routes.

In most programming languages, a loop statement enables an instruction or a collection of statements several times, and below is the basic idea of a loop statement. The C programming language includes the following kinds of loops.

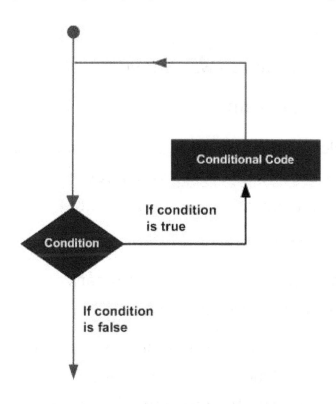

while loop

While loops continue to loop indefinitely until the expression within the parenthesis, (), turns false. The tested variable must be changed, and else the while loop would never end.

do...while loop

The while loop and the do...while loop is similar. The path is verified at the start of the while loop before the content of the iteration is executed.

for loop

A for loop repeats statements a certain number of times. The for-loop parentheses are used to set up, test, and change the loop's control expression.

Nested Loop

The C programming language enables you to nest loops. Loop inside a loop.

Infinite loop

It's a loop that doesn't have a way to end. Therefore it becomes endless.

4.3 Arduino - Functions

Functions enable you to break down the program into smaller chunks of code that accomplish specific functions. When you need to do the same action numerous times in a program, you should create a function.

Organizing source code into functions provides several benefits.

- Functions aid in the programmer's organization. It often helps in the conceptualization of the program.

- Functions codify one operation in one place, reducing the number of times a function should be thought about it and debugged, as well as the number of times the code must be modified.

- Because chunks of code were reused several times, functions make the entire sketch shorter and more compact.

- They make it simpler to buffeted in those other programs by keeping it modular, and they make it more understandable by employing functions.

The loop () and setup () procedures are both necessary inside an Arduino ide or program (). Outside of the brackets of such two functions, new functions must be constructed. The most often used syntax for defining a function is.

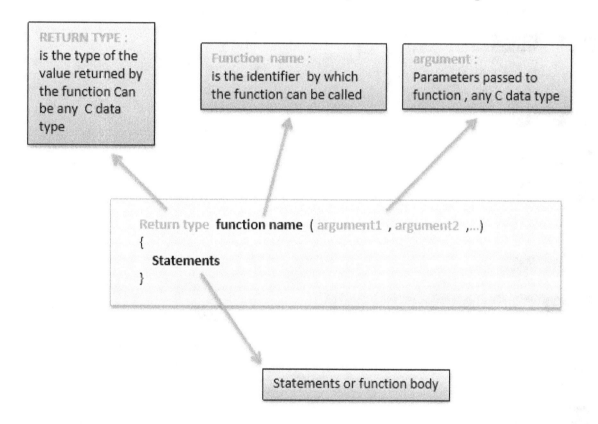

4.4 Function Declaration

A function is defined below or above the loop function, outside of any other functions.

You have two options for declaring the function.

The simplest method is to simply write the component of the function known as a function prototype just above loop function, that consists of the following:

• Function return type

• Function name

• Function argument type (the argument name does not need to be written)

• Function prototype must be followed by a semicolon (;).

The first technique is used to demonstrate the function declaration in the following example.

```
int func_Sum(int a, int b)
{
    int c = 1;
    c = a+b ;
    return c;
}
void setup(){
    Statements Or  set of statements
}
Void loop(){
int result = 0;
result =func_sum(12,12) ;
}
```

The second section, known as the function declaration or definition, must be declared just below the loop function, and it consists of the following elements:

- Function return type

- Function name

- Function argument type (where the argument name must be included).

The body's function (statements in the function where it is calling for executing)

```
int Func_Sub(int a, int b);
void setup(){
A statement or set of statements
}
void loop(){
  int subtraction = 0;
  subtraction = Func_Sub(15,6);
}
int Func_mul(int g, int j)
int q = 0;
q = g*j ;
return q; // return the value
}
```

4.5 Strings

Text is stored using strings. They may be used to show text on an LCD or even in the Serial Monitor window of the Arduino IDE. Strings may also be used to store user input. For instance, the characters which a user writes on an Arduino-connected keypad.

In Arduino programming, there are two sorts of strings:

- Character arrays, which are similar to strings in C programming.

- The Arduino String object, which allows us to utilize the string object in our sketches.

You will learn about strings, objects, and how to utilize them in Arduino projects in this chapter. You'll know which sort of string to utilize in a drawing.

4.6 String Character Arrays

The first sort of string we'll study is a string that consists of a sequence of char characters. You learned how an array is in the last chapter: a sequence of the same data stored in the memory. A string is a collection of character variables. A string is a unique array with an important addition only at the end of a string that is always set to 0. (zero). A "null-ended string" is what this is called.

Example of String Array

```
void setup(){
char exm_str[5];
Serial.begin(9600);
exm_str[0] = 't';
exm_str[1]= 'h';
exm_str[2] = 'e';
exm_str[3] = 'a';
exm_str[4] = 'l';
exm_str[5] = 'i';
Serial.println(exm_str);
```

```
}
void loop() {

}
```

The following example demonstrates how a string comprises a character array containing printable characters with 0 as the array's final member to indicate that the string terminates here. Using Serial. println() and giving the string's name, the string may be printed to the Arduino Serial Monitor window.

```
void setup() {
char exm_str [] = "Hello";
Serial.begin(9600);
Serial.println(exm_str);
}
void loop() {

}
```

The compiler estimates the size of a string array in this sketch and automatically null terminating the string with a zero. The same method is used to build a six-element array comprised of 5 characters preceded by zero, as in the preceding illustration.

4.7 Manipulating String Arrays

As seen in the following sketch, you may change a string array inside a drawing.

```
void setup () {
char love [] = "I love You";
```

```
Serial.begin(9600); // (1) printing the string
Serial.println(love); // (2) deleting the string
love[2] = 0;
Serial.println(love);   //(3) substitute string
love [13] = ' ';
love[18] = 'b'; // insert the new word
love[19] = "o";
love[20] = 'o';
love[21] = k;
Serial.println(love);
}
void loop() {
}
```

Result

I love You

I Love

I Love book

4.8 Manipulate String Arrays

The previous sketch manually altered the string by reading individual characters in it. You may develop your functions or utilize some of the text functions from the C language library to make manipulating string arrays simpler.

String()

The String class, which has been included in the core since version 0019, lets you utilize and modify text strings in more advanced ways than character arrays. Strings may be concatenated, appended to, searched for and replaced with substrings, and more. It consumes greater memory than a plain character array, and it is much more useful.

Character arrays are referenced as strings with a little 's,' while String class instances are referred to as strings with a capital S. Constant strings enclosed in "double quotes" be handled as char arrays rather than String objects.

charAt()

Get a specific character from the String.

compareTo()

Compares two Strings to see whether one is preceding or following the other or equal. The ASCII codes of the characters are used to compare the strings character by character. It indicates that 'a' comes preceding 'B' but after 'A,' for example. Numbers appear first, followed by letters.

concat()

The argument is appended to a String.

c_str()

Converts a string's contents to a null-terminated C-style string. It's worth noting that this provides you direct access to the internal String buffer, so use it with caution. In particular, you must never change the string using the returned reference. Any reference previously given by c str() becomes incorrect and should no longer be utilized when the String object is modified or destroyed.

endsWith()

This function determines if a String terminates with characters from another String.

equals()

Compares two strings to see whether they are equivalent. The string "hello" is not equivalent to the string "HELLO" since the comparison is case-sensitive.

equalsIgnoreCase()

Compares two strings to see whether they are equivalent. The comparison is case-insensitive; thus String("hello") is the same as String("hello") ("HELLO").

getBytes()

The characters of the string are copied to the buffer provided.

indexOf()

Within another String, identifies a character or string. It searches at the start of the string by default, but it may alternatively start at a specific index to find all occurrences of the letter or string.

lastIndexOf()

Within another String, it locates a word or string. It searches from the beginning of the string by default, but it may optionally move backward from a provided index to find all the letter or string occurrences.

length()

It returns the total number of characters in a string.

remove()

Remove characters from the specified index to an end of a string or from specified index till index plus counts in situ.

replace()

Replace all occurrences of a specified character with some other character using the string replace () method. Replace may also be used to replace substrings in a string with another substring.

reserve ()

The String reserve () method enables you to set up a memory buffer for string manipulation.

setCharAt()

Sets one of the string's characters. Has no impact on indices that are longer than the string's current length?

startsWith()

Checks if a string begins with characters from another String.

toCharArray()

The characters of the string are copied to the buffer provided.

substring()

Get a String's substring. The beginning index is inclusive (the substring contains the matching character), while the additional finishing index is exclusive (the corresponding words are not included in the substring). The segment continues to the end of a String if the terminating index is omitted.

toInt()

Converts an integer from a valid String. An integer number should be the first character in the input string. The function will stop converting the string if it includes non-integer integers.

toFloat()

A valid String is converted to afloat. A digit should be the first character in the input string. The function will stop converting the string if it includes non-digit characters. The strings "685.45", "685", and "685fish" are, for example, translated to 685.45, 685.00, and 685.00. It's worth noting that "685.45" is roughly equivalent to 685.45. It's also worth noting that floats only have 6-7 numeric accuracy values, and longer sequences may be truncated.

toLowerCase()

A lowercase form of a Strings is returned. toLowerCase(), as of version 1.0, alters the existing string rather than producing a new one.

toUpperCase()

The upper-case version of the string may be obtained. Instead of creating a new string, toUpperCase() alters the existing one as of version 1.0.

trim()

Have a version of a String that doesn't include any leading or following whitespace. Trim(), as of version 1.0, alters the existing string instead of producing a new one.

4.9 Array Bounds

When working with strings and arrays, it is very important to work within the bounds of strings or arrays. In the example sketch, an array was created, which was 40 characters long, to allocate the memory used to manipulate strings.

If the array were made too small and tried to copy a bigger string than the array, the string would be copied over the end of the array. The memory beyond the end of the array could contain other important data used in the sketch, which our string would then overwrite. If the memory beyond the end of the string is overrun, it could crash the sketch or cause unexpected behavior.

4.10 String Object

The String Object is the second form of text used in Arduino programming.

What is an Object?

A construct that comprises all functions and data is known as an object. A String object may be created and assigned a string or value in the same way as a variable. The String object has functions (also known as "methods" of object-oriented programming (OOP)) that act on the String object's string data.

The accompanying diagram and explanation will demonstrate what an object is or how to utilize the String object.

```
void setup () {

  String my_string= "Object string.";

  Serial.begin(9600);    // (1) print the string

  Serial.println(my_string);   // (2) change the string to upper-case
my_string.toUpperCase();

  Serial.println(my_string);   // (3) string overwrite
my_string = "New object.";

  Serial.println(my_string);

  my_string.replace("Object", "string");

  Serial.println(my_string);
```

```
  Serial.print("Object length is: ");
  Serial.println(my_str.length());
}
void loop() {
}
```

Result

Object string

OBJECT STRING

New Object.

New String.

Object length is 10

A string object is built and given a value (or string) at the top of the sketch. a line

```
my_string= "Object string.";
```

It constructs a String object called my_str and assigns the value "Object string." to it.

It is analogous to defining a variable & assigning it a value, such as an integer.

int My_Num = 108;

The following is how the sketch works.

The string is printed. Like a character array string, the string may be displayed to the Serial Monitor window.

Change the string's case to uppercase. Some various methods or functions may be used on the string object my str that was generated. These methods are called by first typing the object's name, then the dot operator (.), and finally the function's name.

```
My_stringtoUpperCase();
```

The toUpperCase() method turns the string (or text) in the str object of type String to upper-case characters. The Arduino Strings reference contains a list of a function in the String class. A string is technically referred to as a class, and it is utilized to construct String instances.

Overwrite a String

An assignment operator is being used to replace the existing string.

My_string = "New string." with a new string.

Substituting a Word in a String

The replace() method replaces the first string with the second string that is provided to it. Replace () is another String class method that may be used mostly on String object My_string.

Length of the String

Using length to determine the length of the text is simple (). The length() value is delivered straight to Serial. println() in the sample sketch without requiring an intermediary variable.

Use a String Object

A string text array is substantially more difficult to utilize than a String object. The object comes with built-in functions which can manipulate strings in a variety of ways.

The String object's biggest downside is that it consumes an amount of storage and may soon exhaust the Arduino's memory, causing the Arduino to stall, crash, or act strangely. There must be no issues if an Arduino program is modest and restricts the usage of objects.

Text array strings are much more complex to work with, and you may have to build your routines to manipulate them. The benefit is that you can regulate the size of the text arrays you create, allowing you to keep them short and conserve memory.

With string arrays, you must ensure that you do not write past the limits of the array. It is not an issue for the String object, which will take good care of the string boundaries for you whether there is enough space for it to work with. When the String object runs out of memory, it may try to write into memory that doesn't exist, but it will never write beyond the end of the string it's working with.

You learned about strings in this chapter, including how they operate in memory and how to manipulate them.

4.11 Arrays

An array is a data structure of memory regions of the same kind that are arranged logically. The name of an array and the position integer of the individual elements in the array is used to refer to a specific place or element in the array.

An integer array named C with 11 members is shown in the diagram below. You may refer to any of these elements by putting the array name in square brackets, followed by the element's position number ([]). A subscript or index is the official name for the position number (this number specifies the number of elements from the beginning of the array). The initial element is commonly referred to as the zeros element since it bears the subscript 0 (zero).

C[0] (pronounced "C subzero"), C[1], C[2], and so forth are the components of array C. In array C, the maximum subscript is 10, which is less than the array's total number of items (11). The same rules apply to array names as they do to variable names.

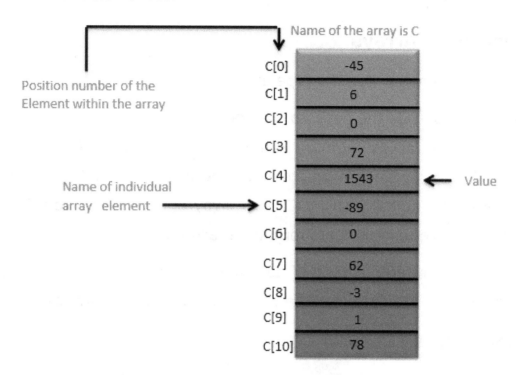

An integer or an integer expression must be used as a subscript (using any integral type). If a system needs an integer as a subscript, the subscript is determined by evaluating the expression. For instance, if variable an equals five and variable b equals 6, two to array item C[11].

An lvalue is a subscripted array name that may be used on the left side of an assignment in the same way as non-array variable names.

Let's take a closer look at array C in the diagram. The complete array is referred to as C. C [0] to C[10] are the 11 components that make up this compound. C[0] has a value of -45, C[1] has a value of 6, C[2] has a value of 0, C[7] has a value of 62, and C[10] has a value of 78.

You would write Serial. Print (C[0] + C[1] + C[2]); to display the total of the values contained during the first three items of array C.

You would write y = C[6] / 2 to divide C[6] by two and result in the variable y.

4.12 Declaring Arrays

Arrays take up memory. Use the type array_Name[]

The compiler sets aside the necessary amount of RAM. (It's worth noting that a declaration that saves memory is more appropriately referred to as a definition.) The array size parameter must be a non-zero integer constant. Use the declaration int C [10]; / C is an array of 10 integers to inform the compiler to reserve ten members for integer array C.

Items of any non-reference type of data may be defined in arrays. An array of type strings, for example, may be used to hold character strings.

4.13 Interrupts

Interrupts cause Arduino's present operation to pause so that other tasks may be completed. Let's pretend you're at home, conversing with someone. The phone suddenly rings. You put down the phone and take it up to talk with the caller. When you've ended your phone discussion, you return to conversing with the person with whom you were conversing before the phone rang.

Similarly, imagine the primary routine as speaking with someone, with the phone ringing interrupting your conversation. The process of chatting on the phone is known as the interrupt service routine. When the phone call is over, you return to your usual talking routine. This example shows how a interrupt forces a processor to respond.

In a circuit, the primary program is running and performs some functions. However, when an interrupt occurs, the main program comes to a stop while another procedure is executed. When these routines are completed, the processor returns to the main Procedure.

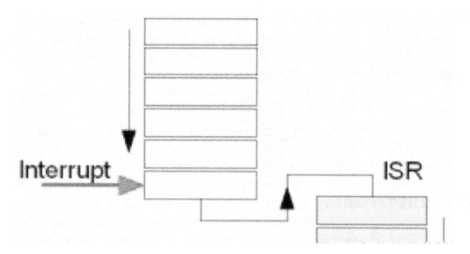

Important features

Here are some key characteristics of interrupts:

- Interruptions may occur from a variety of causes. A hardware interrupt is used in this situation, generated by a state change on one of the digital pins.
- The hardware interrupts "interrupt0" and "interrupt1" are hard-wired to digital I/O pins 3 and 2, respectively, in most Arduino designs.
- The Arduino Mega includes six hardware interrupts, including extra interrupts on pins 21, 20, 19, and 18 ("interrupt2" through "interrupt5").
- A specific function named "Interrupt Service Routine" may be used to create a routine (usually known as ISR).
- You have the option of defining the routine and specifying criteria for the rising, falling, or both edges. The Interrupt would've been served in these circumstances.

- It's feasible to get that function run automatically whenever an event on to an input pin occurs.

4.14 Types of Interrupts

Interrupts are divided into two categories.

- External events, including an alternating voltage pin turning high or low, cause hardware interrupts to occur.
- Software Interrupts happen when a program sends a command to another program. The attach Interrupt () method is the sole sort of Interrupt supported by the "Arduino language."

4.15 Using Interrupts

Interrupts are very important in Arduino applications since they aid in the resolution of timing issues. Reading a rotating encoder or watching a user input is a nice example of utilizing an interrupt. An ISR should, in general, be as brief and quick as feasible. Only one ISR may run at a time if your drawing has several ISRs. Other interruptions will be performed because their priority determines the order after the current one has been completed.

It transmits the data between ISR and the main program, and global variables are often employed. Declare variables shared with an ISR and the primary program as volatile to ensure they are updated appropriately.

The valid values for the three following constants are predefined:

- LOW When the Pin is low, the Interrupt is triggered.
- CHANGE will cause the Interrupt to be triggered the value of the pin changes anytime.
- FALLING: the Pin is moved from a high to a low position.

4.16 Due & Zero

An Arduino Due is an ARM Cortex-M3 board is based upon an Atmel SAM3X8E processor. It will be the first Arduino to use a microprocessor with a 32-bit ARM core.

Important features

- There are 54 digital input/output pins on it (of which 12 can be used as PWM outputs)
- 4 UARTs
- 12 analog inputs (hardware serial ports)
- 84 MHz clock and USB OTG connectivity
- Reset and erase buttons
- 2 DAC (digital into analog), 2 TWI, a voltage connector, an SPI header, and a JTAG header

Communication

UARTs in hardware, 2 I2C, 1 CAN Interfaces (Automotive communication protocol), 1 SPI, 1 JTAG (10 pins) Interface, 1 USB Host (similar to Leonardo), and 1 Programming Port

The Arduino Due board, unlike other Arduino boards, operates at 3.3V. The I/O pins can withstand a maximum voltage of 3.3V. Any I/O pin that receives a voltage greater than 3.3V may be damaged.

The board comes with everything you'll need to get started with the microcontroller. To get started, just plug it into a computer using a micro-USB connection or power it using an AC-to-DC converter or battery. All Arduino shielding that functions at 3.3V is compatible with the Due.

4.17 Arduino Zero

The Zero is a 32-bit expansion of the UNO's platform that is both simple and powerful. The Zero board adds to the family by increasing performance, allowing for a wider range of device projects, and serving as a wonderful instructional tool to learn about 32-bit programming.

Important features

- The board is controlled by Atmel's SAMD21 MCU, which has a 32-bits ARM Cortex M0+ core and may be used for wearable technology, smart IoT devices, high-tech automation, and wacky robots. Atmel's Embedded Debugger (EDBG) is one of its most essential features since it offers a comprehensive debug interface without any need for extra hardware, greatly simplifying software debugging. • EDBG also offers a virtual COM port that may be used for devices and bootloader programming.
- The Zero operates at 3.3V, unlike other Arduino and Genuine boards. The I/O pins can withstand a maximum voltage of 3.3V. Any I/O pin that receives a voltage greater than 3.3V may be damaged.
- The board comes with everything you'll need to get started with the microcontroller. To get started, just plug it into a computer using a micro-USB connection or use an AC-to-DC converter or a battery. All shields that function at 3.3V are compatible with the Zero.

4.18 Arduino – Communication

It facilitates data interchange, dozens of communication protocols are being established. Each protocol may be classified into one of two groups: parallel or serial.

Parallel Communication

For shorter distances of up to a few meters, the parallel circuit between the Arduino with peripheral through i/o ports is the best option. Parallel connection is not practicable in some instances, such as when the conversation between multiple devices must be established across larger distances. Parallel interfaces allow several bits to be sent at the same time. They frequently need data buses, which transfer data across sixteen, twelve, or more wires. The data is sent in massive, crashing waves of 1s and 0s.

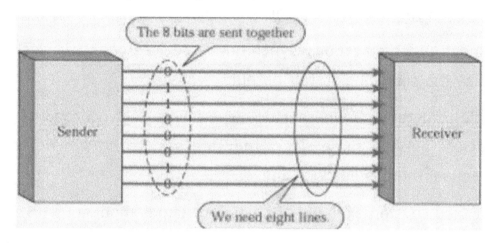

Advantages/ disadvantages

Parallel communication provides a lot of benefits. It's quicker than serial, more intuitive, and simpler to implement. It does, however, need a large number of (I/O) connections and lines. If you've ever had to upgrade a project from a simple Arduino Board to a Mega, you know how valuable and limited the I/O lines on a CPU can be. As a result, You choose serial communication over parallel communication, sacrificing compelling for pin real estate.

Serial Communication

Most Arduino boards now come with a variety of serial connection methods as standard equipment. One of the most crucial aspects of serial communication is the Procedure, which must be followed to the letter. It is just a set of rules for the devices to comprehend the data they communicate appropriately.

Fortunately, Arduino takes care of this automatically, reducing the programmer's/effort users to basic write (data to be transferred) and read operations (received data).

Serial Communications Types

Serial communication is further subdivided into the following categories:

synchronized devices that are synchronized utilize the same schedule, and their time is in sync with one another.

Asynchronous synchronization Asynchronous devices get their clock and are activated by the preceding state's output.

It is simple to determine whether or not a device is synchronous. When all linked devices get the same clock, they are said to be synchronous. It is asynchronous if there is no clock line.

The UART module is an example of an asynchronous module.

There are many built-in rules in the asynchronous serial protocol. These principles are nothing more than methods that aid in the reliable and error-free transmission of data. These mechanics are what You get when You don't use an external clock signal.

Bits of Synchronization

Each data packet contains two or three synchronization bits, which are 2 or 3 special. The start and stop bits are what they're called (s). These bits, as their names suggest, indicate the start and end of a packet.

Only one start bit is always present, but the number of stop bits may be set to 1-2 (though it is normally left at one).

An idle data line traveling from 1 to 0 always indicates the start bit, whereas the stop bit(s) will keep the line at one and return smoothly to the idle state.

synchronicity a few bits

Bits of information

Each packet's data size may be adjusted anywhere between 5 and 9 bits. The usual data size is an 8-bit byte, although another size has its applications as well. When just sending 7-bit ASCII letters, a 7-bits data packet may be more effective than an 8-bit data packet.

Bits of Parity

The user may choose if a parity bit should be present and if the parity should be even or odd. If the amount of 1s in the bytes is even, the parity is 0. Odd parity is the polar opposite of even parity.

Baud Rate (Baud Rate)

The number of bits transmitted per second [bps] is referred to as baud rate. It's important to note that it's talking about bits, not bytes. Each byte must normally be sent with numerous control bits, as dictated by the protocol. It indicates that a single byte in a serial data stream might be 11 bits long. For example, if such baud rate is 300 bps, the maximum and minimum bytes sent per second are 37 and 27, respectively.

Conclusion

My friends, this small book has already come to an end. Although I hope that you will be able to use Arduino programming "off the shelf" in your industry, you will be satisfied if it only stimulates your interest. The techniques outlined in this book are among the most effective ways for Arduino programmers of all levels to improve their performance and expertise. Consider how you and your coworkers will and can utilize them – and other tools that will become available – to boost efficiency. This book is written for Arduino novices and pros who want to learn how to program the board from the ground up. You have attempted to cover the following topic in this book, which is equally important for beginners and professionals.

- Obtain the appropriate Arduino hardware and peripherals for your requirements.

- Download and install the Arduino IDE, then connect it to your Arduino.

- Create, develop, upload, and execute your first Arduino program quickly and easily.

- Understand C grammar, decision-making, strings, data functions and structures

- To operate with memory and prevent typical blunders, use pointers.

- Create development and testing environments, use development and testing shields, and functionality electronics to your Arduino

- Use existing hardware library functions or create your own

- Send output and publish input from analog devices or digital interfaces

- Install an Ethernet shield, install an Ethernet cable, and write a networking program

www.ingramcontent.com/pod-product-compliance
Lightning Source LLC
Chambersburg PA
CBHW082121070326
40690CB00049B/4021